CRAFTING CUMULATIVE SENTENCES

CRAFTING CUMULATIVE SENTENCES

WILLIAM STRONG
Utah State University

RANDOM HOUSE NEW YORK

First Edition
987654321
Copyright © 1984   by Random House, Inc.

All rights reserved under International and Pan-American Copyright Conventions. No part of this
book may be reproduced in any form or by any means, electronic or mechanical, including photo-
copying, without permission in writing from the publisher. All inquiries should be addressed to Random House, Inc., 201 East 50th Street, New York, N.Y. 10022. Published in the United States by
Random House, Inc., and simultaneously in Canada by Random House of Canada Limited, Toronto.

Library of Congress Cataloging in Publication Data

Strong, William, 1940–
   Crafting cumulative sentences.

   1. English language—Sentences.   2. English language—
Composition and exercises.   I. Title.
PE1441.S8   1984   808'.042   83-13805
ISBN: 0-394-33614-3
Manufactured in the United States of America

Text Design by: Dana Kasarsky Design
Illustrations by: Jackie Merritt

for Larry McKinney

A NOTE TO INSTRUCTORS

This book aims to help students explore principles of the "cumulative sentence"—a structure analyzed in detail by the late Francis Christensen in *Notes Toward a New Rhetoric* (New York: Harper & Row, 1967).

Students should not write in this text.

The reasons for *not* writing in the book are both pedagogical and practical: (1) Students learn to write complete sentences by *writing* them, not by "filling in the blanks"; (2) this text can be used by many students if it has not been written in.

The "closure cues" provided with ten exercises following each model sentence are "mental starters"—hints for putting sentences together. They assist students with either oral/choral practice or sentence-level writing in their own notebooks.

Ten "open" exercises follow each model sentence to provide additional practice. Also included is a special section of paragraph-length exercises "decombined" from the prose of eight modern writers. Finally, a section of "generative" exercises concludes the text—this is to provide applied practice with cumulative sentences.

The book's Answer Key enables students to assess their progress in constructing two-level and multilevel sentences and to compare their prose style with professionals, noting similarities and differences.

An Instructor's Manual for the *Sentence Combining in Action* series is available upon request from the College Department at Random House, 201 East 50th Street, New York, NY 10022.

ACKNOWLEDGMENTS

Concepts and exercises in this book derive from the seminal scholarship and outstanding teaching of the late Francis Christensen. In 1968, Francis Christensen took time to challenge my developing ideas about sentence combining—and then introduced me to the research of Kellogg Hunt and John Mellon.

Special thanks go to reviewers of the manuscript for their insightful comments and suggestions: Hugh Burns, United States Air Force Academy; Barbara Gray, Polytechnic Institute of New York; Robert Plec, Oakland Community College; and Richard Tracey, Cerritos Community College. I also want to acknowledge Will Pitkin, William E. Smith, and my colleagues in Secondary Education at Utah State University for their continuing support.

Finally, I am grateful to Steve Pensinger and Steve Young at Random House for their hard work on the *Sentence Combining in Action* series and to my family for shepherding me through it.

CONTENTS

EIGHT MODEST BEGINNINGS 103

ANSWER KEY 113

CRAFTING CUMULATIVE SENTENCES

AN INTRO-DUCTION TO SENTENCE COMBINING

Ever since the late 1960s and early 1970s, a quiet revolution in the way writing is taught has gained momentum. The emphasis has shifted from *taking sentences apart*—the ''grammar approach''—to *putting sentences together*. This new approach is called *sentence combining*—or SC, for short.

SC makes use of what a person already knows about how words go together. Its purpose, simply stated, is to improve a person's skill in constructing clear, correct English sentences. To improve basic writing skills, groups of short, choppy sentences are rewritten into more mature and interesting prose.

SC exercises come in many varieties and formats. What all exercises have in common, however, is the challenge to put given meanings (short sentences) into new, expanded sentence forms called *writeouts*. It's the *practice* in combining—orally ''rehearsing'' possible writeouts, changing word endings or connecting words, reading and rewriting for clarity— that makes the approach so powerful.

Unlike traditional ''dissection'' methods, SC is a natural way to learn about sentences. The aim is not to name sentence parts but to *figure out solutions* to sentence-level problems and to *learn from mistakes*. Mindless combining has no place with the SC approach. The focus is always on *good* writeouts—on making clear and effective meaning.

''STRUCTURED'' VERSUS ''UNSTRUCTURED'' COMBINING

Over the years, a variety of structured hints called *cues* or *signals* have been developed for SC exercises. These cues nudge a person toward constructing sentences in predetermined ways. Structured combining is useful when new or more complex sentence patterns are being introduced.

In contrast, unstructured, or *open*, combining doesn't provide guidance in how to make writeouts. Each person is expected to figure out a few possible solutions and then to select one that *reads best* in context. Open combining is useful when a range of writeouts is being explored.

Both types of exercises are used in the *Sentence Combining in Action* series. To illustrate how both work, let's consider a single SC exercise, approached first in a structured way, then from an open angle. Note that a double numbering system is used. The first number identifies the group of short, related sentences, or the *cluster,* in the exercise; the second number refers to the *sentence* in the cluster.

SENTENCE COMBINING

1.1 Sentence combining is an approach.
1.2 The approach is relatively new.
1.3 The approach is to writing instruction.

2.1 It depends on exercises.
2.2 The exercises are simple.
2.3 Their simplicity is deceptive.

3.1 The challenge is to rewrite sentences.
3.2 The challenge is presented by exercises.
3.3 The sentences are choppy.
3.4 The rewriting is in various ways.

The structured approach presents cues* in the form of partially completed writeouts. The task is to "fill in the blanks" *mentally* with meanings from the SC exercise. With this done, the completed sentences are written out in a separate notebook, *not in the text.*

Attached to cluster 1, for example, the following hints for combining might be given:

1A Sentence combining is a ___________________________________

______________________________________ writing instruction.

1B Sentence ____

______________________________________ relatively new.

1C _______________, an approach _______________________________

_______________, is ____.

By transforming cluster 1 into the above framework, or *sentence frames,* these writeouts should result:

1A *Sentence combining is a relatively new approach to writing instruction.*
1B *Sentence combining is an approach to writing instruction that is relatively new.*
1C *Sentence combining, an approach to writing instruction, is relatively new.*

---

*Note that these cues, derived from the powerful psycholinguistic principle of *closure,* represent a simple, natural way to teach syntax. Since the human mind is predisposed to "fill in" grammatical patterns, there seems little need to set up a complex signaling system of graphic triggers and cue words to prompt "target" transformations. Closure cues also teach punctuation patterns inductively.

Here are sentence frames for cluster 2:

2A It ____

that are ____________________________________ simple.

2B It ____

____________________________________ exercises.

2C It ____________________________________ exercises

that are ________________in their ____________________.

Writeouts should look like this:

2A *It depends on exercises that are deceptively simple.*
2B *It depends on deceptively simple exercises.*
2C *It depends on exercises that are deceptive in their simplicity.*

For the third cluster, consider the following sentence frames:

3A The challenge ____________________________ is

____ ways.

3B To rewrite ________________________________

is the challenge ____________________________.

3C Exercises present the challenge of ________________

____.

Clearly, the cues for cluster 3 introduce more complex writeouts.

3A *The challenge presented by exercises is to rewrite choppy sentences in various ways.*
3B *To rewrite choppy sentences in various ways is the challenge presented by exercises.*
3C *Exercises present the challenge of rewriting choppy sentences in various ways.*

With the options written out, a person then selects one sentence from each group to put into a final paragraph. Here are writeouts 1A, 2A, and 3A in the form of a paragraph.

Sentence combining is a relatively new approach to writing instruction. It depends on exercises that are deceptively simple. The challenge presented by exercises is to rewrite choppy sentences in various ways.

MORE SENTENCE OPTIONS

The open approach to combining involves the same process of creating sentence options and making choices—but no hints are provided. The whole point of the unstructured approach, after all, is to explore a broad range of sentence possibilities. As each person switches on an internal guidance system—and compares writeouts with others produced in class—new strength in writing develops. Here are some open SC clusters:

4.1 Each cluster represents a possible writeout.
4.2 The cluster is short sentences.
4.3 A writeout is a transformation.
4.4 The transformation is "more mature."

5.1 But clusters can also be combined.
5.2 They can be divided.
5.3 They can be left as is.

6.1 The aim is not long sentences.
6.2 The sentences are convoluted.
6.3 The sentences are difficult to read.
6.4 The aim is good ones.
6.5 They express meanings clearly.

In approaching such exercises, it's helpful to first identify a *base* sentence—the sentence in a cluster that contains the main focus of meaning. We let this base sentence serve as a foundation and then work left-to-right *through* it, adding information and rearranging phrases so that the writeout "sounds right." Whispering sentences aloud, hearing an "inner voice"—these are absolute basics for successful combining practice, not to mention successful writing.

For cluster 4, the first sentence—*Each cluster represents a possible writeout*—can serve as the foundation. Let's add meanings from the rest of the cluster to produce three writeouts:

4A *Each cluster of short sentences represents a possible writeout; this writeout is a transformation that is "more mature."*

4B   *Each cluster of short sentences represents a possible writeout—a "more mature" transformation.*

4C   *A possible writeout—that is, a "more mature" transformation—is represented by each cluster of short sentences.*

Cluster 5 is quite straightforward in its possibilities. Notice the contrast between writeouts 5A and 5B in stylistic effect. Then study how writeout 5C integrates meanings from clusters 4 and 5.

5A   *But clusters can also be combined or divided—or they can be left as is.*

5B   *But clusters can also be combined, divided, or left as is.*

5C   *Each cluster of short sentences represents a possible writeout—a "more mature" transformation—but clusters can also be combined, divided, or left as is.*

With cluster 6, there are many stylistic options. Here are three for consideration:

6A   *The aim is not long, convoluted, or difficult-to-read sentences; the aim is good ones, with clearly expressed meanings.*

6B   *The aim is not long sentences—convoluted or difficult to read—but good ones that express meanings clearly.*

6C   *The aim is good sentences and clear expression of meanings, not sentences that are long, convoluted, or difficult to read.*

The task of choosing the "best" writeout from available options is not an easy one. Sentence variety is an important principle to keep in mind. Perhaps the best advice is to *read sentences aloud*—and to make choices on the basis of "fit" with preceding sentences in a paragraph.

Here is one set of choices that consciously employs the principle of sentence variety:

Each cluster of short sentences represents a possible writeout—a "more mature" transformation—but clusters can also be combined, divided, or left as is. The aim is not long, convoluted, or difficult-to-read sentences; the aim is good ones, with clearly expressed meanings.

A WORD ABOUT MISTAKES

Many people are afraid to write because they are afraid of making mistakes. Sentence combining is a way to reduce this fear. Because the content of writing is provided by exercises, a person can focus undivided attention on making clear, correct sentences. Fear is naturally reduced as sentence-making skills improve.

It's important to regard mistakes for what they really are—opportunities to learn. How else can a person learn to walk, talk, or write except by making countless mistakes? A mistake is nothing to be ashamed of; it's a necessary part of learning—a focus for future practice. The goal is to learn from mistakes, not to repeat them.

Some mistakes in combining result from carelessness. A person may occasionally misspell words from an exercise or leave out capital letters at the beginning of sentences. Other mistakes result from bad habits. A person may routinely drop the *'s* on possessive forms of nouns or use expressions carried over from conversational speech (for example, *This sentence combining, it really works*).

Let's suppose that a person has trouble making complete sentences from SC exercises. Faced with an SC cluster, the person produces this writeout—a *sentence fragment*:

> *Each cluster of short sentences representing a possible writeout, which is a "more mature" transformation.*

A sentence fragment exists when a piece of a sentence is punctuated as if it were a complete sentence. Such a problem results from *not hearing* how the sentence should sound. One solution is to divide the original cluster into smaller chunks for combining; this brings the writeout more under control.

> *Each cluster of short sentences represents a possible writeout. A writeout is a transformation that is "more mature."*

The person must realize that the *-ing* verb form (*representing*) is "incomplete." By repeatedly comparing complete sentences with fragments, this realization will develop.

A related (and more common) problem is the *run-on* sentence:

> *But clusters can also be combined, they can also be divided or left as is.*

A run-on sentence exists when two separate sentences have been "run together" with a comma. This error results from *not hearing* the two separate sentences. Once the problem is labeled and recognized, various solutions can be routinely practiced. First, a period or semicolon can be substituted for the comma; then the sentence can be rewritten—in this case to conclude with a series:

But clusters can also be combined, divided, or left as is.

Out-of-place phrases or incorrect word forms are a third kind of mistake. These give rise to awkwardness or confusion:

The aim is not sentences that are long, convoluted, or difficult to read; the aim is clearly expressed meanings, which are good sentences.

While the first half of the preceding sentence reads fine, the second half sounds scrambled or "out of control." The solution involves saying the sentence aloud slowly, *thinking* about meaning, and making the second part follow the expected pattern:

The aim is not sentences that are long, convoluted, or difficult to read; the aim is good sentences, which have clearly expressed meanings.

In summary: Taking chances with language, trying new things with sentences, will inevitably result in a certain level of mistakes. A person who is confronted with an overwhelming number of mistakes should work with simpler types of combining until basic skills are better established.

SC practice brings mistakes out in the open so that a person can *learn* from them. For this reason, mistakes should be welcomed and carefully studied. Each mistake conquered is a threshold that a person crosses—another step toward mature skills and increased self-confidence in writing.

THE CUMULATIVE SENTENCE

Skill in writing is something you *learn,* not something you're born with. You learn writing—just as you learn many other skills—by practicing it until it seems a "natural" part of who you are.

The learning-by-doing process in this book is a very straightforward one. First you'll be given a model sentence that has been broken down into levels so that you can see how it is built. Then you'll imitate this model by doing sentence-combining exercises. Finally, you'll practice making similar kinds of sentences on your own and apply what you have learned in new contexts.

If you have already flipped through the text, you may well be asking yourself: What *is* a cumulative sentence? Why study it? How does it differ from other patterns such as simple, compound, or complex sentences?* Let's briefly consider these three questions.

The cumulative sentence is usually constructed with a main thought put first and the details—typically, phrases and clauses—coming later. It is a flexible, loosely structured sentence; in fact, its parts can often be moved around for stylistic effect or emphasis. Detail is not so much worked *into* the sentence as *added to* it.

Because the cumulative sentence is a tool used by many modern writers, it probably deserves your close study. This is not to say, of course, that professional writers use *only* cumulative sentences; this would be roughly equivalent to restricting yourself only to backhand shots on the tennis court. The point is that the cumulative sentence will *extend* your repertoire of language skills.

You will soon learn that the typical cumulative sentence is built on the foundation of a *simple sentence.* Later in this book, you will also see that details can be added in cumulative style to *compound sentences.* Although *complex sentences* have not been used in this text as foundations for cumulative patterns, they certainly could be. Here the basics are being emphasized.

You should focus on the *clarity* of cumulative sentences, not merely on their length. Complexity in itself is no virtue. A related point pertains to the use of cumulative sentences in your own writing. Don't *overdo* a good thing. Think about purpose and audience as you begin to tinker

---

*A *simple sentence,* or *independent clause,* consists of a subject and a predicate; both of these sentence parts may be compound (joined by words such as *and, but, or, nor*). A *compound sentence* consists of two or more independent clauses; these are also connected by coordinating conjunctions (*and, but, or nor, for, yet,* and sometimes *so*). A *complex* sentence consists of one independent clause and one or more *dependent* clauses; subordinating conjunctions (such as *because, when, if, although,* etc.) and relative pronouns (such as *who, whom, which, that,* etc.) are the connecting words.

with your prose style—and remember that shorter is sometimes better. Brevity has force.

BACKGROUND CONCEPTS

Before getting into model sentences, let's first consider the idea of levels. The base sentence is usually at a *general* level, and additions to the sentence are usually more *specific*. Looking at a sentence in terms of its levels is simply a way of understanding how details modify (or relate to) more general parts. Remember that *general* and *specific* are relative terms.

Consider, for example, the following pairs of words. Ask yourself: Which is general and which is specific? Label the general words *1* and the specific words *2*.

   ___2___ motorcycle / vehicle ___1___

   _______ fuel / gasoline   _______

   _______ salmon / fish   _______

   _______ color / magenta   _______

   _______ pumpkin / vegetable _______

Compare your answers with these:

1	2
2	1
1	2
2	1

Let's try the same kind of exercise with phrases, just to make sure that the concepts of general and specific are clear.

   ___1___ misplaced clothing / old buckle boots ___2___
   _______ bull riding / important rodeo event   _______
   _______ reasons for laughing / good grades   _______
   _______ significant decision / who you marry   _______
   _______ gypsies stole homework / lame excuse _______

Your answers should look like these:

```
2       1
1       2
1       2
2       1
```

Returning to general and specific words, let's now consider them in clusters rather than in pairs. The task, as illustrated here, is to rearrange words into a general-to-specific order. Each successive level is indented.

Ford   **1** automobiles

automobiles   **2** Ford

Mustang   **3** Mustang

oats   **1** _______________

grain   **2** _______________

food   **3** _______________

entertainment   **1** _______________

Star Wars   **2** _______________

movies   **3** _______________

rage   **1** _______________

emotions   **2** _______________

anger   **3** _______________

essay   **1** _______________

writing   **2** _______________

communication   **3** _______________

editorial   **4** _______________

Here are the answers to the preceding exercise:

1 food
  2 grain
    3 oats
1 entertainment
  2 movies
    3 *Star Wars*

1 emotions
  2 anger
    3 rage
1 communication
  2 writing
    3 essay
      4 editorial

Our next step is to number successive levels of specificity with phrases. This time, however, some of the items will be equally general or equally specific. When this occurs, you should repeat the numbering for a given level. Study the illustration that follows:

death of loved one	**1**	life's sorrows
life's sorrows	**2**	death of loved one
breakup of family	**2**	breakup of family

delicious desserts	**1**	__________
banana split	**2**	__________
fresh apple pie	**2**	__________

water sports	**1**	__________
sailing competitively	**2**	__________
summer recreation	**3**	__________

costs considerable money	**1**	__________
harmful to health	**2**	__________
reasons for not smoking	**2**	__________
stains teeth	**2**	__________

capitalist countries	**1**	__________
communist countries	**2**	__________
U.S.A.	**2**	__________

Soviet Union	**1**	__________
China	**2**	__________
Canada	**2**	__________

Your answers to the preceding exercise should read as follows:

1 delicious desserts
  2 banana split
  2 fresh apple pie
1 summer recreation
  2 water sports
    3 sailing competitively
1 reasons for not smoking
  2 costs considerable money
  2 harmful to health
  2 stains teeth
1 capitalist countries
  2 U.S.A.
  2 Canada
1 communist countries
  2 Soviet Union
  2 China

THE SIMPLE CUMULATIVE SENTENCE

The concepts of general and specific sentence levels apply directly to the *cumulative sentence*. As you have already seen, a general word or phrase is like an aerial photographic view. It provides an overview—an inclusive "big picture"—of ideas being covered verbally. On the other hand, a specific word or phrase is more like a photographic closeup. It "fills in" a detail of the larger view. A cumulative sentence is one that has both an "overview" part, or level, and more specific, detailed parts.

In each of the three examples that follow, general and specific sentences are combined to make a simple cumulative sentence.

The classroom was quiet.   (general)
Students waited expectantly.   (specific)

1   ***The classroom was quiet,***
    2   with students waiting expectantly.   (cumulative)

> ***They sat hunched in unison.***   (general)
> Their elbows were on their desk tops.   (specific)

1 ***They sat hunched in unison,***
    2 elbows on their desk tops.   (cumulative)

> ***Rain spattered the windowpane.***   (general)
> It made trickling rivers on the glass.   (specific)

1 ***Rain spattered the windowpane,***
    2 making trickling rivers on the glass.   (cumulative)

What these cumulative sentences have in common is a more general base sentence (set in boldface for ease of identification) and a more specific *free modifier* (indented to show its relation to the base sentence). Each of these parts, general and specific, is numbered. These numbers are referred to as *levels*.

As you can see, a *free modifier* is a phrase or clause structure—a group of words (or "chunk" of meaning) derived from a sentence.* To make a sentence into a free modifier, you delete words and/or change verb forms (for example, from an *-ed* ending to an *-ing* ending):

SENTENCE   **FREE MODIFIER**

Students waited expectantly.⟶with students waiting expectantly

Their elbows were on their⟶elbows on their desktops
desktops.

It made trickling rivers on the⟶making trickling rivers on the
glass.   glass

With some constructions you also add a connecting word (such as *with*) to the free modifier.

In short, you might think of a free modifier as any less-than-sentence "chunk" of meaning that can be grammatically added to an existing sentence to make the resulting writeout more clear, detailed, or specific. As you will later note, free modifiers can be attached *before*, *within*, or *after* complete sentences. Remember, however, that the posi-

---

*Earlier you were introduced to the term *sentence fragment*. Note that a fragment is nothing but a free modifier punctuated as a sentence. Free modifiers, or fragments, cannot stand by themselves as complete, independent clauses—except for deliberate stylistic effect. Generally, they are rewritten *into* sentences or *attached to* sentences.

tioning of free modifiers is not a completely open-ended matter. Certain constraints—such as the position (or meaning) of words being modified—sometimes demand that free modifiers be repositioned so that the final writeout makes sense.

The point of studying levels in sentences is to understand how sentence parts interlock in regular, patterned ways. The aim, ultimately, is to select what you want to emphasize as your base sentence and then to attach various modifiers to express meanings as clearly and fully as possible.

Getting comfortable with levels involves imitating certain sentence models. You should realize, however, that these models are not necessarily ''better'' than sentences you're already able to make. The value of a sentence, after all, depends on *context*—on where and how it's used. What the models offer you are new options with words, helping you to write with more authority and flexibility.

In studying and practicing various forms of the cumulative sentence, remember that such sentences should be used *sparingly* in the real writing that you do. Quality in writing depends more on *variety* in sentence length and structure than on mere complexity.

THE TWO-LEVEL SENTENCE

The cumulative sentence has two basic subtypes: the two-level sentence and the multilevel sentence. A *two-level sentence* has a base sentence plus two or more of the same level of free modifier. To understand the difference between a noncumulative sentence and a two-level sentence, we will compare two writeouts from the same cluster of short sentences:

> **Harold shuffled to the front of the room.**
> He knotted his shoulders tensely.
> He jammed his hands into his pockets.

First, let's make a writeout that has all its parts at level 1—the base sentence level.

NONCUMULATIVE SENTENCE

1   *Harold shuffled to the front of the room, knotted his shoulders tensely, and jammed his hands into his pockets.*

Now we'll make a second writeout—a two-level sentence—in which details modify the base sentence, making it more specific.

CUMULATIVE SENTENCE (TWO-LEVEL)

1   *Harold shuffled to the front of the room,*
   2   knotting his shoulders tensely,
   2   jamming his hands into his pockets.

In the first example, the noncumulative sentence is clear and well written, but its parts are all at the *same level* of generality. Why? Because it is simply a series of actions—like separate snapshots—based on a time sequence: first, Harold shuffles; then he knots his shoulders; then he jams his hands into his pockets. The two-level sentence, on the other hand, is a bit more subtle. It says that one general action is occurring but that more specific actions are occurring *simultaneously—as part of* the larger action.

With the noncumulative sentence, then, you see three general pictures of Harold. With the cumulative sentence, however, you have one general picture plus two "closeups" that give details about the larger action. The advantage of the cumulative sentence, quite simply, is that it can help you describe more accurately the way things are in reality.

In the example of a two-level sentence, notice the parts: a general base sentence (boldfaced level 1) and free modifiers that amplify the base sentence. The sentence is "two-level" because both of its free modifiers have the same grammatical pattern:

knott*ing* his shoulders tensely,
jamm*ing* his hands into his pockets.

You may be wondering if more second-level modifiers can be added. The answer is yes. As the following example makes clear, the result is still a two-level sentence:

1   *Harold shuffled to the front of the room,*
   2   knotting his shoulders tensely,
   2   jamming his hands into his pockets,
   2   scowling at the chalkboard, and
   2   muttering to himself.

Notice that the additional free modifiers repeat the *-ing* pattern and add further details to the base sentence (level 1).

To see how free modifiers can be moved to another position—*in front of* the base sentence—study the following example carefully. Notice how free modifiers keep the same *-ing* pattern; notice also that one free modifier has become part of the base sentence.

MODIFIERS BEFORE AND AFTER BASE SENTENCE

Knotting his shoulders tensely, jamming his hands into his pockets, **Harold shuffled to the front of the room and muttered to himself,** scowling at the chalkboard.

2   Knotting his shoulders tensely,
2   jamming his hands into his pockets,
1   **Harold shuffled to the front of the room and muttered to himself,**
2   scowling at the chalkboard.

To see how free modifiers can be moved *within* the base sentence as well as *in front of* it, consider the next example:

MODIFIERS BEFORE AND WITHIN BASE SENTENCE

Muttering to himself, **Harold shuffled to the front of the room—** knotting his shoulders tensely, jamming his hands into his pockets— **and scowled at the chalkboard.**

2   Muttering to himself,
1   **Harold shuffled to the front of the room—** / —**and scowled at the chalkboard.**
/2/   knotting his shoulders tensely,
/2/   jamming his hands into his pockets

As you study this example, pay particular attention to the analysis of levels. A slash mark (/) is used to show where free modifiers occur *within* the base sentence.

Here's a summary of main points that have been covered so far:

1. A *cumulative sentence* consists of a general statement—a base sentence—plus more specific parts called free modifiers, which are like photographic "closeups." Such a sentence enables you to show simultaneously both the "big picture" and key details.
2. As a type of cumulative sentence, the *two-level sentence* has two components: a general statement plus free modifiers that each repeat the same grammatical pattern. These modifiers can occur *before, within,* or *after* the base sentence.

OTHER FREE MODIFIERS

So far, the focus has been on one kind of free modifier—the *-ing* type. There are other kinds, of course. Let's scan some possibilities for free modifiers, remembering that being able to *use* them does not necessarily mean that you have to memorize their grammatical labels. These various modifiers are ones that you'll be practicing later.

VERB CLUSTERS (-*ING* PARTICIPLES)—*modifiers whose verbs, when changed to -ing form, modify a noun in the base sentence*

Harold sneered disdainfully.
Harold shuffled to the front of the room.
Harold played a "tough guy" role.

Sneering disdainfully, **Harold shuffled to the front of the room,** playing a "tough guy" role.

  2   Sneering disdainfully,
1 **Harold shuffled to the front of the room,**
  2   playing a "tough guy" role.

VERB CLUSTERS (*-ED PARTICIPLES*)—*modifiers whose verbs, used in -ed form, modify a noun in the base sentence*

He was bored with the discussion.
He was annoyed by his instructor's request.
He turned to face the class.

Bored with the discussion and annoyed by his instructor's request,
he turned to face the class.

2 Bored with the discussion and
2 annoyed by his instructor's request,
1 **he turned to face the class.**

NOUN CLUSTERS (APPOSITIVES)—*modifiers that define or rename a noun in the base sentence*

Harold's scowl was leveled at the chalkboard.
The scowl was a look of rebellion.
The chalkboard was a horizon full of scribbles.

Harold's scowl—a look of rebellion—**was leveled at the chalkboard,** a horizon full of scribbles.

1 **Harold's scowl— / —was leveled at the chalkboard,**
/2/ a look of rebellion
2 a horizon full of scribbles.

ADJECTIVE CLUSTERS—*modifiers that describe a noun in the base sentence*

His emotions were smoldering.

His emotions were fierce.
His emotions were red hot.
His emotions were ready to be ignited.

↓

His emotions were smoldering—fierce, red hot, ready to be ignited.

↓

1   ***His emotions were smoldering***—
2   fierce,
2   red hot,
2   ready to be ignited.

ABSOLUTES—*modifiers that modify an entire base sentence*

His lips were pulled back.
His teeth were clenched.
He muttered to himself.

↓

With his lips pulled back, his teeth clenched, **he muttered to himself.**

↓

2   With his lips pulled back,
2   his teeth clenched,
1   **he muttered to himself.**

So much for examples of free modifiers. All such modifiers can be put *before*, *within*, or *after* the base sentence.

THE MULTILEVEL SENTENCE

A multilevel sentence is a cumulative sentence containing a base sentence and free modifiers that don't repeat the same grammatical pattern. Instead, *different* types of free modifiers are added to the base sentence. (The types are the same ones you noted above: (1) verb clusters; (2) noun clusters; (3) adjective clusters; and (4) absolutes.) Each successive level or modifier tends to become more specific, more detailed.

To better understand the difference between a noncumulative sentence and a multilevel sentence, we'll make two writeouts from the same cluster of sentences:

Harold shifted his weight self-consciously.
Harold stood before the class.
His face was flushed.
His brow exploded with perspiration.

Here is a noncumulative sentence—one with its parts all at the same level.

NONCUMULATIVE SENTENCE

1   *Harold shifted his weight self-consciously and stood before the class;*
1   *his face was flushed, and his brow exploded with perspiration.*

And here is a multilevel sentence for contrast:

CUMULATIVE SENTENCE (MULTILEVEL)

2   Shifting his weight self-consciously,
1   *Harold stood before the class,*
      3   his face flushed,
      3   his brow exploding with perspiration.

As you can see, the noncumulative sentence—though vivid and effective—is like separate snapshots set before the reader. The cumulative sentence is more like a *moving* picture, with the general and specific parts integrated.

Notice that *two* types of modifiers are used in the preceding multilevel sentence. The first modifier (level 2) is a verb cluster; the other modifiers (level 3) are absolutes. *Every time you change the grammatical pattern, you shift to a new level.* Notice also that there are *two* level 3 modifiers. Why? *Because like patterns stay at the same level.*

To tell whether modifiers are alike or different, you should read them aloud and study how they look. The following free modifiers, for example, are clearly different patterns:

> barely audible
> a gurgling whisper

Not surprisingly, therefore, these free modifiers will be at different levels in a multilevel sentence:

> Harold's voice was barely audible.
> **Harold's voice was a murmur.**
> The murmur was a whisper.
> The whisper gurgled.

Barely audible, **Harold's voice was a murmur,** a gurgling whisper.

> 2   Barely audible,
> 1   **Harold's voice was a murmur,**
> 3   a gurgling whisper.

Study the following free modifiers to determine which two are most alike in grammatical form.

> its silence building
> its tension breathless
> a dramatization of "student in trouble"

Clearly, the first two free modifiers have a similar pattern—and differ from the third free modifier. Here's how these modifiers would look in a multilevel sentence:

> **Then the class applauded Harold's effort.**
> Its silence was building.
> Its tension was breathless.
> His effort was a dramatization of "student in trouble."

Then the class—its silence building, its tension breathless—**applauded Harold's effort,** a dramatization of "student in trouble."

1   *Then the class— / —applauded Harold's effort,*
      /**2**/   its silence building,
      /**2**/   its tension breathless
         3   a dramatization of "student in trouble."

Notice once again that the slash mark (/) indicates where the two free modifiers are inserted *into* the base sentence.

For a final illustration of the multilevel sentence, examine the following free modifiers. Which two seem to be the same type?

    grinning with satisfaction
    chest thrust forward
    thumbs hooked in his belt loops

To check your hunch that the first free modifier differs from the second two, study them in the context of a multilevel sentence.

    He grinned with satisfaction.
    He swaggered toward his desk.
    His chest was thrust forward.
    His thumbs were hooked in his belt loops.

    Grinning with satisfaction, **he swaggered toward his desk**—chest thrust forward, thumbs hooked in his belt loops.

    2   Grinning with satisfaction,
1   **he swaggered toward his desk—**
      3   chest thrust forward,
      3   thumbs hooked in his belt loops.

CONCLUSION

As you work through the exercises that follow, remember that whether sentences have two or more levels, the parts go together in very regular ways. Once you get comfortable with the basic patterns, you'll be able to construct cumulative sentences on your own without struggling with their structure.

Here are some hints about how to get the most from exercises in this booklet:

1. Study the model sentence in each section, reading it aloud so that you can hear its rhythm and fix in your mind its pattern of levels.
2. Look at an exercise cluster, seeing how you can fit its parts together with the boldfaced base sentence as your "foundation."
3. Using the cues provided, transform the short sentences into a two-level or multilevel sentence that is somewhat *like* the model but certainly not identical to it; *write out complete sentences in your own notebook, not in the text.*
4. With a model clearly in mind, try your hand at some of the open combining exercises that follow each section.
5. Put the booklet aside and make your *own* sentences, following the patterns you have been practicing.
6. Try doing open exercises in the second section of the text, "Eight Modern Writers," comparing your prose with that of professionals.
7. Move on to the third section of the text, "Eight Modest Beginnings," and use the base sentences there to generate details for various types of free modifiers and/or new sentences.
8. In the paragraphs created from "Eight Modest Beginnings," concentrate on having a *balance* between short, simple sentences and longer ones in a cumulative style.

The point of all these suggestions is for you to transfer what you've learned to your real writing. Toward this end, you will find it helpful to rewrite sentences in some of your drafts, working for *variety* in sentence length and structure—a clear, balanced style. The goal, remember, is *good* sentences, not long ones.

EIGHT MODEL SENTENCES

MODEL A: TWO-LEVEL SENTENCE

(MODIFIERS AFTER BASE SENTENCE)

The driver wheeled her van.
The wheeling was near the freight dock.
The driver squinted against the sun.
The sun was setting.
The driver checked her mirrors.
The mirrors were for rear view.

The driver wheeled her van near the freight dock, squinting against
the setting sun, checking her rear-view mirrors.

1   **The driver wheeled her van near the freight dock,**
  2   squinting against the setting sun,
  2   checking her rear-view mirrors.

A•1   Terry glanced at Tonya.
The glance was desperate.
Terry was looking for help.
The help was on a question.

1 Terry ____,

    2 looking _______________________________________.

A·2 *The player took the handoff.*
The player turned sharply.
The player faked to the outside.
The player rolled against tacklers.

1 ____,

    2 turning ______________________________________,

    2 faking _______________________________________,

    2 ____.

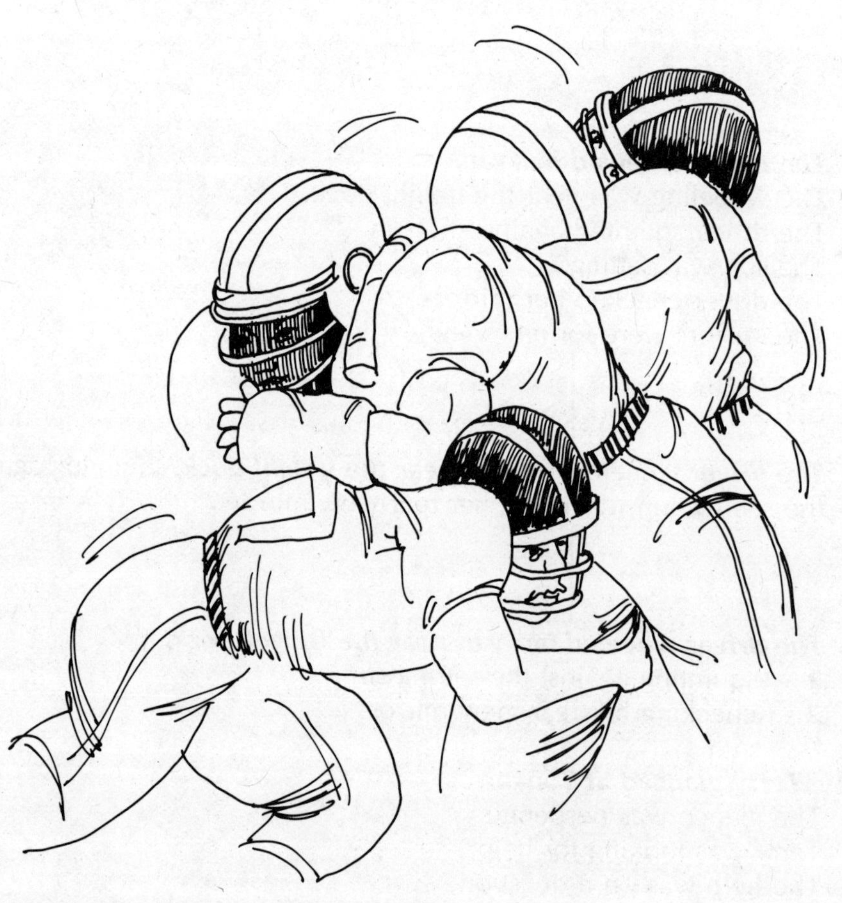

A•3 *The dancer was at the window.*
The dancer was slender.
The window was rain-smeared.
She watched the traffic.
She thought about her boyfriend.

1 ____ ,

2 ____ ,

2 thinking _______________________________________ .

A•4 *Shouts echoed through the courtyard.*
The shouts were shrill.
The shouts were discordant.
The shouts were full of emotion.
The emotion was churning.

1 Shouts ____ —

2 _______________________ and ___________________ ,

2 full ____ .

A•5 *Lennon's music was a force.*
The force was political.
It was a voice.
The voice was sensitive.
The voice spoke for millions.

1 ____ ,

2 a sensitive voice ______________________________ .

A•6 *Two girls elbow into line.*
Their legs are long.
Their skirts are short.
Their talk is slangy.
Their talk is bright.

1 ____ —

2 their legs long,

2 their ____ ,

2 their ____ .

A·7 ***We sat quietly in the darkness.***
The darkness was oppressive.
We were huddled together for warmth.
We were troubled by noises.
The noises came from outside.

1 ____,

    2   huddled ______________________________________,

    2 ____.

A·8 ***The job seeker comes in.***
The job seeker is inexperienced.
He blinks with embarrassment.
He licks his lips nervously.
He fumbles with words.

1 ____,

    2   blinking ______________________________________,

    2 ____,

    2 ____.

A·9 ***The flag is a symbol.***
It is a focus for ceremonies.
The ceremonies are social.
It is a means of uniting people.
The unification is momentary.

1 ____

    2   a focus ______________________________________,

    2   a means ______________________________________.

A·10 ***The skier came over a crest.***
The crest was low.
The crest was choppy.
Her body was crouched.
Her weight was forward.
One ski was slightly ahead of the other.

1 ____

2   her ____,

2   her ____,

2   one ski slightly ahead of the other.

MODEL A: ON - YOUR - OWN EXERCISES

A•11   *The instructor approached our group.*
He was smiling affably.
He was trying to look sincere.

A•12   *Writing well requires effort.*
The effort is a sustained concentration.
The concentration is mental.

A•13   *The sky was a cobalt blue.*
It was utterly clear.
It was brutally cold.

A•14   *She headed in his direction.*
Her walk was quick.
Her face was angry.

A•15   *Ours is a nation of hope.*
It is a land of opportunity.
The opportunity is for immigrants.
The immigrants are homeless.

A•16   *The stranger moved into the sunshine.*
The sunshine was brilliant.
His hands were on his hips.
A hat was pulled low over his eyes.

A•17   *And then shouts erupted.*
The shouts were savage.
The shouts were bloodthirsty.
The shouts were full of hate.

A•18   *Debbie inspects her mirror image.*
She first puffs up her hairdo.
Her hairdo is a "beehive bouffant."
She then replasters her lipstick.
Her lipstick is ruby red.

A•19   *Missiles nestle in their concrete silos.*
The missiles are intercontinental.
The missiles are both here and abroad.
Their systems are programmed.
Their warheads are armed.

A•20 *Nurses have a program of study.*
The program is highly demanding.
The program includes course work.
The program includes internships.
The program includes examinations.
The examinations are comprehensive.

MODEL B:
TWO-LEVEL SENTENCE
(MODIFIERS BEFORE BASE SENTENCE)

The teacher smiled to himself.
The teacher erased the board.
The erasing was with a sweep.
The sweep was lazy.
The teacher trailed patterns of chalkdust.
The chalkdust was gritty.
The chalkdust was grayish.

Smiling to himself, erasing the board with a lazy sweep, **the teacher trailed patterns of gritty, grayish chalkdust.**

2   Smiling to himself,
2   erasing the board with a lazy sweep,
1   **the teacher trailed patterns of gritty, grayish chalkdust.**

B•1   Mark closed his eyes.
Mark slumped at his desk.
Mark hoped to catch a quick nap.

2   Closing _______________________________,

2   _______________________________,

1   Mark _______________________________.

B•2   The future is rich with promise.
The future is abundant with opportunity.
The future lies before us.

2   Rich _______________________________,

2   _______________________________,

1   the future _______________________________.

B•3   The salesman was suave.
The salesman was cunning.
The salesman was eager to make a buck.
The salesman sidled near to his prey.

2   _______________________________,

2   _______________________________,

2   eager to make a buck,

1   the salesman _______________________________.

B•4   Molly's face was angry.
Molly's mouth was twitching in disgust.
Molly stood her ground.
The stand was defiant.

2   Her face angry,

2   her _______________________________,

1   Molly _______________________________.

B•5   The car careened out of the lot.
The lot was vacant.
The car weaved from side to side.
The car rumbled down the alley.
The alley was deserted.

2   _______________________________,

2   weaving _______________________________,

1   _______________________________.

B·6   The present moment sparks with life.
The present moment crackles with possibilities.
The possibilities are untried.
The possibilities are untested.
The present moment feels electric.

2   ____,

2   ____,

1   the present moment ____________________________.

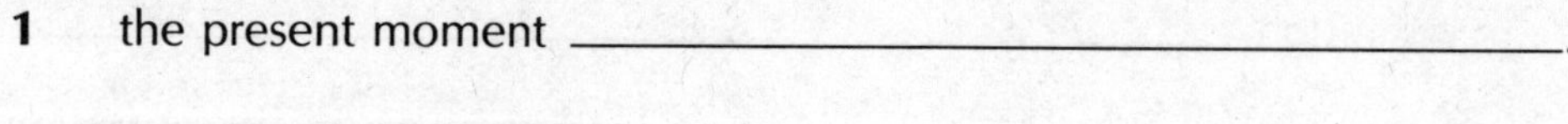

B•7   Senator Snort is a defender of liberty.
Senator Snort is a spokesperson for minorities.
Senator Snort is a fiscal conservative.
Senator Snort is a friend of the environment.
Senator Snort deserves your support.

2   A defender _________________________ ,

2   _________________________ ,

2   _________________________ ,

2   _________________________ ,

1   Senator Snort _________________________ .

B•8   The lecture hall was painted green.
The lecture hall was stuffed with desks.
The desks were scarred.
The lecture hall was a waiting room.
The waiting room was institutional.

2   Painted _________________ and _________________ ,

1   _________________________ .

B•9   The old man's body was bent.
The old man's body was frail.
His walk was shuffling.
His walk was labored.
The old man moved down the sidewalk.

2   His body bent and _________________________ ,

2   his walk _________________________ ,

1   the old man _________________________ .

B•10   Jill was unaware of the danger.
She would soon face the danger.
Jill was anxious to reach the summit.
Jill climbed toward an outcropping.
The outcropping was rocky.
The outcropping was warmed by the sun.

2 Unaware ________________________________

________________________________,

2 ________________________________,

1 Jill ________________________________

________________________________.

MODEL B: ON-YOUR-OWN EXERCISES

B•11 The tree swayed dangerously.
The tree groaned in protest.
The tree withstood high winds.

B•12 Mr. Thomas was quite elderly.
Mr. Thomas was unable to care for himself.
Mr. Thomas finally moved to a retirement home.

B•13 The gift was an act of love.
The gift was a gesture of kindness.
The gift went unacknowledged.

B•14 One eye was closed.
The other was squinting fiercely.
Janice slowly squeezed the trigger.

B•15 I was comfortable with sentence combining.
I was eager to try my skills.
I decided to make my own sentence.
The sentence was two level.

B•16 The committee worked together.
The committee stuck to the business at hand.
The committee refused to squabble.
The committee soon finished its task.

B•17 The legislator was sincere in his efforts.
The legislator was misguided in his approach.
The legislator campaigned on his record.
His record was remarkably ineffectual.
He lost the election by a landslide.

B•18 George was a skilled craftsman.
George was a fine athlete.
George was a terrific cook.
George won a community award.
The award was for being "well rounded."

B•19 Minorities were encouraged by gains.
The gains were during the civil-rights era.
Minorities have consolidated their clout.
Minorities have become a potent force.
The force is in American politics.

B·20   Her voice was lyrical.
Her voice was pure.
Her interpretation was sensitive.
Her interpretation was compelling.
The singer made her debut.
The debut was in New York.

MODEL C: TWO-LEVEL SENTENCE
(MODIFIERS WITHIN BASE SENTENCE)

Rock music burst from the speakers.
The music was loud.
The music was harsh.
The music was primitive.

$$\downarrow$$

Rock music—loud, harsh, and primitive—*burst from the speakers.*

$$\downarrow$$

1   *Rock music— / —burst from the speakers.*
   /2/   loud,
   /2/   harsh, and
   /2/   primitive

C•1 *Jean felt her pulse quicken.*
   Jean listened hard.
   Jean heard unusual noises.

1   Jean— / —felt _______________________________.
   /2/   listening _______________________________,
   /2/ _______________________________

C•2 *Inflation undermines the stability of government.*
Inflation is the devaluation of currency.
Inflation is the erosion of buying power.

1   Inflation— / —undermines _________________________.

   /2/   the devaluation _________________________,

   /2/   the erosion _________________________

C•3 *A study group debates various possibilities.*
The group examines the problem.
The group struggles with options.

1   A study group— / —debates _________________________.

   /2/   _________________________,

   /2/   struggling _________________________

C•4 *Mud oozed between her toes.*
The mud was warm.
The mud was relaxing.

1   _________________________— / —oozed between her toes.

   /2/   _________________________ and _________________________

C•5 *The quarterback drops back to pass.*
One arm is cocked.
The other is extended for protection.

1   _________________________— / —drops back to pass.

   /2/   one arm cocked,

   /2/   _________________________

C•6 *Storm waves thundered against the rocks.*
They exploded into foam.
They spewed white up the cliffs.
The cliffs were jagged.

1   Storm waves— / — _________________________.

   /2/   exploding _________________________,

   /2/   _________________________

C·7 *The cabin now belonged to him.*
The cabin was damp.
The cabin was creaky.
The cabin was badly in need of cleaning.

1   The cabin— / —____.
/2/ damp,

/2/ ____,

/2/ ____

C·8 *The school's priorities were clear to its staff.*
The priorities were athletics.
The priorities were social events.
The priorities were a marching band.

1 ________________________________— / —were clear to its staff.

/2/ ____,

/2/ ____,

/2/   a marching band

C•9 *Power lines stretch through the desert.*
The lines run parallel to the road.
The lines span gulches.
The lines span streambeds.
The streambeds are rocky.

1 Power lines— / — _______________________________.

/2/   running _________________________________,

/2/ ____

C•10 *The team captain approached the podium.*
His neck was reddened above his collar.
The collar was white.
His shoulders were flexing for the girls.
His shoulders were muscular.

1 _______________________________— / —approached the podium.

/2/ ____,

/2/   his muscular shoulders flexing _____________________

MODEL C: ON-YOUR-OWN EXERCISES

C•11 *The football took a great bounce.*
The football was kicked end-over-end.
The bounce was in the wrong direction.

C•12 *Our product is ready to market.*
It is thoroughly tested.
It is fully guaranteed.

C•13 *The driver careened into the ditch.*
The driver glanced down carelessly.
The driver reached for a cigarette.

C•14 *A broken cup was all that remained.*
Its handle was missing.
Its rim was badly chipped.

C•15 *Theresa headed for the campus job office.*
She heard about summer opportunities.
The opportunities were for employment.
The employment was in national parks.

C•16 *The company's goals have been achieved.*
The goals are reduced expenses.
The goals are increased sales.
The goals are higher profits.

C•17 *Many women share housework.*
They are reluctant to give up careers.
They are reluctant to give up interests.
The interests are intellectual.
The sharing is with their husbands.

C•18 *American companies are now producing cars.*
The companies are responding to Japan's challenge.
The companies are trying to regain leadership.
The cars are highly fuel-efficient.
The cars are much more reliable.

C•19 *The hurricane gathered force.*
It was the second of the season.
It was a storm with tremendous fury.
The force was destructive.
The gathering was 500 miles offshore.

C•20   *A group of coal miners marches in protest.*
Their banners are uplifted.
Their arms are locked together.
The protest is silent.
The protest is against safety conditions.
The safety conditions demand attention.

MODEL D: TWO-LEVEL SENTENCE
(MODIFIERS IN TWO POSITIONS)

The average worker struggles against inflation.
The average worker battles a tax burden.
The average worker is "on the defensive."
The average worker tries to consolidate gains.
The average worker tries to minimize losses.

Struggling against inflation, battling a tax burden, ***the average worker is "on the defensive,"*** trying to consolidate gains and minimize losses.

2   Struggling against inflation,
2   battling a tax burden,
1   ***the average worker is "on the defensive,"***
2   trying to consolidate gains and minimize losses.

D•1   He raced the engine.
He slipped the machine into gear.
He backed carelessly across the sidewalk.

    2   Racing ____________________________________

1   he _______________________________________ ,

    2   backing __________________________________ .

D•2 The coach was wearing a school blazer.
The coach stood before the crowd.
The coach was grinning good naturedly.

    2   Wearing ______________________________ ,

1   the coach ________________________________ ,

    2   ____ .

D•3 Fireworks were like flowers in a garden.
Fireworks blossomed briefly in space.
Space was the night sky above the river.

    2   Like __________________________________ ,

1   fireworks ________________________________ ,

    2   the night sky ___________________________ .

D·4   The reporter was down near the action.
The reporter got out her notepad.
The reporter was ready to record the details.

2   Down ________________________________ ,

1   ________________________________ ,

2   ready ________________________________ .

D·5   They were surprised by the turnout.
They hesitated for a moment.
They were hunched in a doorway.

2   ________________________________ ,

1   ________________________________ ,

2   hunched ________________________________ .

D·6   ***The sky was edged by trees.***
The sky was an enormous blue hole.
The trees were a circle of green.

1   The sky— / —was edged ________________________________ ,

/2/   an ________________________________

2   a circle ________________________________ .

D·7   ***Hawkins angled toward the baseline.***
Hawkins was a forward.
The forward was lanky.
The baseline was an unguarded area.

1   Hawkins— / —angled ________________________________ ,

/2/   a ________________________________

2   an ________________________________ .

D·8   The afternoon was golden.
The afternoon was warm.
The afternoon was like a dream.
The dream was breathless with promise.

2   ________________________________ and ________________________________ ,

1   the afternoon ________________________________ ,

2   breathless ________________________________ .

D•9 *The room was decorated in yellows and earth tones.*
The room was a small vestibule.
This was a happy mix of colors.

1   The room— / —was decorated _______________________________

____,

   /2/   a ____

   2   a ____.

D•10 *Clouds had formed a storm front.*
The clouds were gray on the horizon.
The clouds were sullen on the horizon.
The storm front was ominous in its portent.

1   Clouds— / —had formed _______________________________,

   /2/   _______________ and _______________________________

   ____

   2   ominous ____.

MODEL D: ON-YOUR-OWN EXERCISES

D•11   Jeff listened to the cheers.
Jeff stepped to the plate.
Jeff eyed the center-field bleachers.

D•12   I was glad for the experience.
I drove back home after the tournament.
I was now confident in my ability.

D•13   The republic was flirting with disaster.
The republic had overextended itself.
The republic was borrowing at high interest rates.

D•14   Both arms were extended.
She vaulted across the balance beam.
Her timing was perfect.

D•15   The bomb was a harmless-looking package.
The bomb ticked away toward noon.
Noon was the fateful hour.
The hour would wreak destruction.

D•16   *The young woman appeared suicidal.*
She was listless.
She was distraught.
She appeared unable to cope.

D•17   Officials were nervous about their investment.
Officials were reluctant to pull out their money.
Officials waited anxiously for news.
They were hopeful for a major oil find.

D•18   *The wrestler grinned at the crowd.*
The wrestler was a perfect villain.
The crowd was a collection of farm hands.
The farm hands liked a good show.
The show was on a Saturday night.

D•19   *Her house was on the edge of town.*
It was an old, brick Victorian.
It had begun to decay from neglect.
This was a place where the asphalt ended.
This was a place where crab grass took over.

D·20 The convict did not expect reprieve.
The convict did not want reprieve.
The convict faced his death with dignity.
He tried to atone for his crimes.
The crimes were violent.
The crimes had caused much suffering.

MODEL E: MULTILEVEL SENTENCE
(MODIFIERS AFTER BASE SENTENCE)

The wingman hurtled down the ice.
The wingman was raw boned.
His skates were flashing.
The puck was cradled by his stick.
He forced the goalie to come out.

The raw-boned wingman hurtled down the ice—his skates flashing, the puck cradled by his stick—forcing the goalie to come out.

1   **The raw-boned wingman hurtled down the ice—**
  2   his skates flashing.
  2   the puck cradled by his stick—
    3   forcing the goalie to come out.

E·1   **The singer stepped into the footlights.**
  He grinned down at the girls.
  His mouth formed a kiss.

1   The singer ________________________________ ,

    2   grinning ________________________________ ,

        3   his mouth forming ________________________ .

E•2   *Election results come in slowly.*
The small precincts report first.
They provide data for predictions.

1   ________________________________ ,

    2   the small precincts reporting first,

        3   providing ________________________ .

E•3   *Dancers moved in syncopation.*
They were nodding.
They were jerking.
Their faces were transfixed.

1   Dancers ________________________________ ,

    2   ________________ and ________________ ,

        3   their faces ________________________ .

E•4   *The cat came with a leap.*
The cat was tan.
The cat was tawny.
The cat sprang on its prey.

1   The cat _________________________________,

2   ______________ and ___________________,

    3   springing ___________________________.

E•5   *She was tall and gaunt.*
She was shimmering in sequins.
Her face was frozen in a smile.
The smile was waxy.

1   She was _______________ and _________________,

2   ________________________________ —

    3   her ____________________________.

E•6   *Mike lifted the tone arm.*
The tone arm was copper colored.
Its needle was delicate.
It was poised above the record.
The record was grooved.

1   Mike _______________________________,

2   _____________________________________,

    3   poised ___________________________.

E•7   *It was a sanctuary.*
It was a place of refuge.
It was cool.
It was quiet.
It was away from telephones.

1   It _________________________________,

2   a _______________________________ —

    3   _______________________________,

    3   _______________________________,

    3   _______________________________.

E•8   *Most children begin school with enthusiasm.*
They are eager to learn.
They are open to knowledge.

They literally hunger for stimulation.
The stimulation is intellectual.

1 ____ —

  2 eager ____ ,

  2 ____ —

    3 literally _______________________________________

    ____ .

E•9 *Life is thin and tensile.*
Life is a stream of consciousness.
The consciousness sparks between Alpha and Omega.
Alpha and Omega are the cosmic poles.
The poles are positive and negative.

1 ____ ,

  2 a stream of consciousness _____________________________

  ____ ,

    3 the positive and negative ____________________________

    ____ .

E•10 *There was a single image.*
The image was his father.
His father was heavy muscled.
His father was beaded with sweat.
His father turned to smile at him.
His father turned to wave at him.

1 There ____ —

  2 his ____ —
    3 heavy muscled,

    3 ____ ,

      4 turning _____________________________________

      ____ .

MODEL E: ON-YOUR-OWN EXERCISES

E•11 *Our coach leaps from the bench.*
He gestures wildly at the referee.
His face is a portrait of anguish.

E•12 *The moon hung in the night sky.*
It was a crescent of pale light.
It was distant and sad.

E•13 *Friends came in hordes.*
Their voices were full of cheer.
They were singing ballads.

E•14 *The commission was a public-relations effort.*
It was symbolic but meaningless.
Its recommendations were a joke.

E•15 *Sue stood in the lunch line.*
She was hungry for dessert.
She thought about her commitment.
The commitment was to lose weight.

E•16 *Music is an escape.*
The escape is a magic journey.
The journey takes us into ourselves.
It provides a brief vacation.

E•17 *Footsteps retreat slowly.*
They scuff across linoleum.
The linoleum is sandy.
The linoleum is well worn.
Their sound finally fades.

E•18 *Then came an announcement.*
The announcement was inane.
It was the fourth of the period.
It caused our instructor to groan.
It caused our instructor to curse.

E•19 *The carriage lumbers forward.*
Its wheels are glinting in the sun.
Its chassis is straining under its load.
The load is a heap of scrap metal.
The metal is badly rusted.

E•20   *The old barn shuddered.*
Its walls were buckling.
They collapsed with a roar.
They sent up sparks in a shower.
The shower was like a flurry of fireflies.
The fireflies went rising in the night.

MODEL F: MULTILEVEL SENTENCE
(MODIFIERS BEFORE AND AFTER BASE SENTENCE)

The motorcycle throbbed heavily.
The motorcycle idled in the sunshine.
The motorcycle was lean.
The motorcycle was dechromed.
The motorcycle was poised for acceleration.

Throbbing heavily, ***the motorcycle idled in the sunshine***—lean and dechromed—poised for acceleration.

    2   Throbbing heavily,
1 ***the motorcycle idled in the sunshine***—
      3   lean and dechromed—
        4   poised for acceleration.

F•1   She was awake again.
He squinted at the typewriter keys.
They were knotted against the carriage roller.

2   Awake ________________________________,

1   he ________________________________,

    3   knotted ________________________________.

F·2   The hair was like wisps of cobwebs.
Rick's hair was combed straight back.
This gave him a severe appearance.

    2   Like ________________________________,

1   ________________________________,

    3   giving ________________________________.

F·3   The willows dipped at the wind's bidding.
The willows swayed dramatically.
Their branches danced in rhythm.

    2   Dipping ________________________________,

1   ________________________________,

    3   branches dancing ________________________________.

F·4   The stew was a rich mix of vegetables.
The stew bubbled in the pot.
The stew attracted people by its smell.

    2   A ________________________________,

1   ________________________________,

    3   attracting ________________________________.

F·5   Two students laughed wildly.
Two students waited at the bus stop.
One swang his arms in pantomime.
The other made strange faces.

    2   Laughing ________________________________,

1   ________________________________—

    3   one swinging ________________________________

________________________________,

    3   the other ________________________________

________________________________.

F•6   The paper ball made a neat trajectory.
The paper ball bounced against overdue books.
It skittered into an open briefcase.
The briefcase was a kind of wastebasket.

    2   Making ________________________________ ,

1   ____ ,

    2   skittering ________________________________ ,

        3   a ________________________________ .

F•7   The rig was grimy from hours on the road.
The rig was parked near a café.
Its exhaust soot spread in a black banner.
The soot feathered out near the rear door.

    2   Grimy ________________________________ ,

1   ____ ,

        3   its exhaust soot spreading ________________

____ ,

        4   feathering ________________________________

____ .

F•8   Chris is alert.
Chris is aggressive.
Chris searches for answers.
Chris probes beneath the surface.
Chris seeks hidden truths.

    2   ________________________ and ________________ ,

1   ____ ,

        3   probing ________________________________ ,

        3   ____ .

F•9   Railroad passenger service is outdated by aircraft.
Railroad passenger service is expensive to operate.
Railroad passenger service must make changes.
It must improve its coaches.
It must serve good food.
It must treat its customers courteously.

    2   Outdated _______________________________________,

    2   _______________________________________,

1   railroad passenger service _______________________________

        3   improving _______________________________,

        3   _______________________________,

        3   _______________________________.

F•10   SAC is armed.
SAC is ready.
SAC is on twenty-four-hour alert.
Its planes are lined up.
Its pilots are directed toward targets.
Its backup systems are in order.

    2   _______________________ and _______________,

1 SAC is _______________________________—

    3 its planes _______________________________,

    3 _______________________________,

    3 _______________________________.

MODEL F: ON-YOUR-OWN EXERCISES

F•11   A friendship is like money in the bank.
A friendship is something you draw upon.
It helps you get through hard times.

F•12   The executive was aging gracefully.
The executive now seemed more relaxed.
The executive seemed a little less defensive.

F•13   Dawn eased light across the land.
Dawn came quietly in the east.
Its progress was soft and inexorable.

F•14   The economy was battered by recession.
The economy finally began to regain strength.
This made investors feel more confident.

F•15   The typist was eager to please his boss.
The typist took evening classes.
He boosted his speed.
The speed became 100 words per minute.

F•16   We hoped to get the contract.
We presented our analysis.
The analysis was a projection of trends.
The trends were for consumer demand.

F•17   The building was devoid of ornament.
The building was clean, angular, and contemporary.
It was a stark glass box.

F•18   I was out of breath.
I was late again for class.
I ran down the hallway.
The hallway was now deserted.
I did not know what to expect.

F•19   The team captain leans toward the camera.
The team captain stands at the sidelines.
He is thick shouldered.
The sidelines are a roped-off area.
He looks shy and confused.

F•20 The women were huddled together.
Their hands were in their jackets.
The women rocked with laughter.
Their voices were loud.
Their voices were clear.
They were sharing more than recipes.

MODEL G: COMPOUND TWO-LEVEL SENTENCE

(TWO BASE SENTENCES WITH TWO-LEVEL MODIFIERS)

So far, you have studied sentences with one base clause (level 1). In the next two sections of exercises (Models G and H), matters will get slightly more complex as you try your hand at *compound sentences*—those with *two* base clauses to which free modifiers can be attached. (Actually, however, these sections are merely a review of the principles that you have already learned.) Sentences become compound when two clauses are linked with a *coordinating conjunction (and, but, or, for, nor, yet, and sometimes so)*. Typically, a comma precedes these coordinating conjunctions to signal a pause. The following examples illustrate the compounding of two base sentences.

PHIL: I never use coordinating conjunctions, so I never make compound sentences.

JILL: Either you are lying, or you are trying to make a bad joke.

PHIL: I like simple sentences, but I absolutely loathe compound ones.

JILL: Your words may be strongly spoken, yet their structure contradicts their content.

PHIL: Well, it's my opinion, and it's very true.

JILL: (Sigh)

The band of workers grinned at the tourists.
The band of workers settled in.
The workers did construction.
They winked.
They swaggered back and forth.
They waited for the action.
The police came.
Their handcuffs were ready.

AND THEN

Grinning at the tourists, ***the band of construction workers settled in***—winking, swaggering back and forth, waiting for the action—***and then the police came,*** their handcuffs ready.

2   Grinning at the tourists,
1   *the band of construction workers settled in*—
   2   winking,
   2   swaggering back and forth,
   2   waiting for the action—
1   *and then the police came,*
   2   their handcuffs ready.

G•1

The music was loud.
The music was glittering with guitars.
The dancers moved with the sound.
Their bodies were jerking.
Their hips were grinding.
Their hips were gyrating.
Their feet were pawing the floor.

AND

1   The music _________________________________,

   2   glittering _________________________________,

1   and the dancers _________________________________—

   2   their bodies jerking,

   2   their _______________ and _______________,

   2   _________________________________.

G·2 Some students are docile.
Some students are passive.
⎯ **Some students refuse to take responsibility.**
AND The responsibility is for learning.
⎣ **The system finally "educates" them.**

The system helps them to "adjust."
The system encourages them to "fit in."
The system encourages them not to ask questions.

2 _________________________________ and _________________________,

1 some students ____

____,

1 and the system ____ —

  2 helping ____,

  2 encouraging _____________________________________

____.

G•3

AND

  Smog hung over the city.
Smog choked off the light.
The light was from the sun.
All the heat seemed trapped.
The heat mixed with dirt.
The heat mixed with waste.
The waste was industrial.
The heat made the air unbearable.

1 Smog ____,

  2 choking ____,

1 and all the heat— / —seemed trapped,

  /2/ mixed ____

____

  2 making ____.

G•4

BUT

  A beard keeps one's face warm.
A beard protects one's face.
The protection is from the cold.
A beard shields one's face.
The shielding is from the wind.
It also attracts attention.

It sometimes lends credence.
The credence is to one's arguments.

1 ____—

    2   protecting ________________________________,

    2   shielding ________________________________—

1   but it ________________________________,

    2 ________________________________.

G•5

    Many of Sutton's poems are dead.
BUT His lines are buried in geography.
    His words are muffled in cliché.
    This poem is alive.
    This poem is engaging.
    This poem forces the reader to listen.
    This poem demands a response.

1 ____—

    2   his lines buried ________________________,

    2   his ________________________________—

1   but this poem is ______________ and ______________,

    2 ________________________________

    and demanding ________________________________.

G•6

    The optimist sees things as hopeful.
WHEREAS *The optimist sees things as exciting.*
    The things seem rich with promise.
    The pessimist sees things as dark.
    The pessimist sees things as impossible.
    The things seem absurd.
    The absurdity is hopeless.

1   The optimist ________________________________

as ________________ and ________________________ ,

2   rich ________________________________ ,

1   whereas ________________________________

as ________________ and ________________________ ,

2   ________________________________ .

G•7   The jet lifted into the horizon.
┌── ***The jet powered upward.***
**AND
THEN**   The jet was a Boeing 747.
└── ***It banked to the east.***
Its skin glinted.
The skin was silver.
Its shape got smaller.
Its roar faded.

2   Lifting ________________________________ ,

1   the jet— / —________________________________ ,

/2/ ________________________________

1   ________________ it banked ________________________ ,

2   its ________________________ glinting,

2   its ________________ getting ________________________ ,

2   its ________________________________ .

G•8
┌── ***Everyone worked together.***
**AND
THEN**   Everyone pushed in unison.
Everyone rocked the car.
└── ***It slowly began to edge forward.***
The wheels were spinning.
The wheels were catching hold.
The engine was revving in protest.
The protest was unmuffled.

1 Everyone ________________________________—

2 ________________________________,

2 rocking ________________________________—

1 ________________________________,

2 wheels ________________ and ________________,

2 engine ________________________________.

G•9   The poet works at odd hours.

The poet pores over notebooks.
The poet pores through papers.
AND   The poet tries to get organized.
The poet hopes for an idea.
Sometimes the sentence happens.
The sentence is perfect.
The sentence is a window.
The window is into another universe.

 2   Working ______________________________ ,

1   ______________________________ —

 2   ______________________________ ,

 2   hoping ______________________________ —

1   and sometimes ______________________________ ,

 2   a window ______________________________ .

G·10   Norton was a misfit.
    Norton was an oddball.
    Norton was a crackpot.
    Norton tried to promote legislation.
BUT   The legislation was for a 6:00 P.M. curfew.
    His efforts were unsuccessful.
    This was thanks to a citizens' group.
    The group rose up in protest.

 2   A ______________ , an ______________ , and a ______________ ,

1   Norton tried ______________________________

    ______________________________ ,

1   but ______________________________ ,

 2   ______________________________

    ______________________________ .

MODEL G: ON-YOUR-OWN EXERCISES

G•11   *A voice spoke to him.*
The voice was soft.
The voice was forgiving.
He hung up the phone without reply.

G•12   *The signal changes color.*
Cabbies race to the next intersection.
They gun their engines unmercifully.
They honk their horns.

G•13   We wanted to beat the crowds.
We hoped to get a front-row seat.
We took a shortcut to the stadium.
So did everyone else in town.

G•14   The peasants were brutalized by war.
The peasants desperately wanted peace.
Their leaders had other ideas.
Their leaders were insulated from suffering.

G•15   *Girls were lying on the grass.*
They were eating sandwiches.
They were sipping milkshakes.
Boys were swaggering down the walk.
They were trying to look *macho.*

G•16   *The officer stared straight ahead.*
She was assessing the threat.
Then she moved down the aisle.
Her heels were clicking on the tile.
Her weapon was drawn.

G•17   *Christmas is a time for joy.*
It is a season for giving.
For many it brings depression.
Depression is an inner ache.
The ache is called loneliness.

G•18   He listened to the sermon.
He mulled over its message.
The message was guilt laden.
The words seemed suddenly hollow.
They seemed empty of meaning.

G•19 The shout was unrestrained.
The shout was jubilant.
A shout went up from the crowd.
The marathon winner stumbled toward the finish.
Her arms were lifted in victory.
Tears were streaming down her face.

G•20 ***The earth revolves around the sun.***
It completes a cycle every 365¼ days.
It also rotates on its axis.
This rotation is every 24 hours.
This gives us day and night.
This is a framework for our lives.

MODEL H: COMPOUND MULTILEVEL SENTENCE
(TWO BASE SENTENCES WITH MULTILEVEL MODIFIERS)

AND THEN

The students were very quiet.
The children stared at their books.
Their hands were folded in their laps.
The teacher jumped to his feet.
He shouted with surprise.
His face was bright with rage.
One hand rubbed his bottom.
His bottom was tack stung.

The students were very quiet—staring at their books, their hands folded in their laps—**and then the teacher jumped to his feet,** shouting with surprise, his face bright with rage, one hand rubbing his tack-stung bottom.

1 **The students were very quiet—**
  2   staring at their books,
    3   their hands folded in their laps—
1 **and then the teacher jumped to his feet,**
  2   shouting with surprise,
    3   his face bright with rage,
    3   one hand rubbing his tack-stung bottom.

H•1

Tony put his razor on the sink.
The sink was a bowl of porcelain.
AND THEN
The bowl was shallow.
The bowl was squarish.
He closed his eyes.
He cupped his hands together.
He splashed water on his face.

1   Tony _______________________________,

    2   a bowl _______________________________,

      3 _______________ and _______________,

1   and then he _______________________________,

    2 _______________________________,

    2   splashing _______________________________.

H•2 Jennifer was intrigued by the grasshopper.

Jennifer eyed it carefully.
BUT THEN
She watched its struggle for escape.
Her mother called her to lunch.
Her mother was the voice of authority.
The call broke the spell.

    2   Intrigued _______________________________,

1   Jennifer _______________________________,

      3   watching _______________________________,

1   but then her mother— / —called her to lunch,

   /2/   the voice _______________________________

      3   breaking _______________________________.

H•3 A buzzer was loud.
A buzzer was abrasive.

┌── *A buzzer echoed up the hall.*
AND   It was a signal for school to begin.
└── *Students raced for their classes.*
   Their shirttails were flying.
   Their books were tucked under their arms.

2 ________________________________ and ________________,

1 ____,

   3   a signal ______________________________________,

1 and students ______________________________________,

   2   their ____,

   2   books tucked ________________________________.

H•4   The teenager prayed for a reprieve.

       The teenager switched to evasive techniques.
       The techniques included giggles.
BUT The techniques included small talk.
       The small talk was disjointed.
       The parent leaned forward.
       Her manner was insistent.
       She probed for straight answers.

      2   Praying ________________________________,

1   ________________________________—

        3   ________ and disjointed ________—

1   but the parent ________________________,

      2   her ________________________,

        3   probing ________________________.

H•5   The clam diggers dragged their gunny sacks.

       The clam diggers were ghostly shapes.
       Their movements were slow.
       Their movements were meditative.
BUT They were hunched in the wind.
       They were hunched in the fog.
       All of this would change by noon.
       Noon was a rendezvous time for surfers.

      2   Dragging ________________________,

1   ________________________________—

        3   their movements ________________

           ________________________________,

          4   hunched ________________________

           ________________________________—

1   but all of this ________________________,

      2   a ________________________________.

H·6   The diver took his leap.

AND THEN
- *The diver sprang high into the air.*
- His arms were outstretched.
- His silhouette was like a bird's.
- *He tucked in a slow roll.*
- His body was in rhythm.
- The rhythm was perfect.
- He knifed the water.

   2   Taking _________________________________,

1   ____—

      3   his arms _______________________________,

      3   his silhouette like _____________________—

1   and then ______________________________,

   2   his body _______________________________,

      3   knifing ______________________________.

H·7   The pusher is afraid of doing without.

AND THUS
- *The pusher works the streets.*
- The pusher hustles drugs.
- The hustling is to support his habit.
- *The circle of addiction widens.*
- The circle engulfs the young.
- The circle entices the gullible.

   2   Afraid ________________________________,

1   ____,

      3   hustling ______________________________

      ____,

1   and thus ______________________________,

   2   engulfing _____________________________

   2   ____.

H•8   The clouds churn with energy.
The clouds come rolling in.
The clouds are sullen.
AND   The clouds are dark.
Their shapes are like mushrooms.
The wind becomes ominous.
The wind brings a sound.
The sound is turbulent.
The sound is a memory of other storms.

2   Churning _________________________,

1   _________________________,

3   _________________ and _____________,

4   their shapes _________________,

1   _________________________,

2   bringing _________________,

3   a memory _________________.

H•9   Aunt Grace hovers over the stove.
Her hair is in curlers.
Aunt Grace sets out her cup.
Aunt Grace measures out a teaspoonful.
AND THEN   The teaspoonful is coffee.
The coffee is instant.
She pours the water.
The water is a stream.
The stream sizzles.
The stream consumes the crystals.

2   Hovering _________________,

3   her hair _________________,

1   _________________________,

2   measuring _________________,

1   _________________________,

2   a sizzling stream _________________.

H•10

Compassion is such a simple act.
It is a matter of smiling.
It is a matter of listening.

YET   It is showing concern.
The concern is for another person.
It is offering a helping hand.
We often have trouble.
The trouble is conquering the fears.
The fears keep us apart.

1 _______________________________________—

2 a matter of _________________ and _________________,

3 showing _________________________________

or offering _________________________________—

1 ____

____.

MODEL H: ON-YOUR-OWN EXERCISES

H•11 *The coffee was now cold.*
He pushed it across the counter.
He stared at its bracken color.
The color was a disagreeable brown.

H•12 *Traffic moved smoothly until dusk.*
Then the winter storm hit.
It made the streets treacherous.
It made the streets inhospitable.
This was a bonanza for tow-truck operators.

H•13 Monique is a feminist.
Monique often attends rallies.
She speaks about women's issues.
She maintains a low profile at work.
She refuses to be baited into argument.

H•14 The play is upbeat.
The play is funny.
The play is irreverent.
The play rivets one's attention.
It provokes thought through humor.
It also allows one to relax.

H•15 *He pulled out on the highway.*
He waited for the traffic to clear.
Then he pushed on the accelerator.
He left two "autographs."
The "autographs" were a signature.
The signature was familiar.

H•16 *Children race across the field.*
They shriek.
They whoop wildly.
They are glad to be on vacation.
Then they hit the water.
They pelt each other with mud.

H•17 *The engine converts combustion into energy.*
The engine is fueled by gasoline.
The crankshaft transfers this energy to the axle.
The energy is called "torque."
This makes the wheels turn.
This causes the car to move.

H•18   The students are anxious to record ideas.
The ideas are their writing instructor's.
The students wait.
Their notebooks are open.
Their pencils are poised.
Unfortunately a substitute arrives.

H•19   Her confidence was up.
The batter tensed with anticipation.
She toed the dust.
Then she connected with a fast ball.
She sent it into left field.
This was a game-winning hit.

H•20   The Frisbee is flicked sideways.
The Frisbee soars.
It spins in an upward trajectory.
It slices the horizon.
Then it hovers.
It is silent and graceful.
It rides a puddle of air.

EIGHT MODERN WRITERS

Sentence-combining exercises in this section derive from the published prose of skilled modern writers. No cues for combining are provided. Your task is to combine the clusters in ways that make sense to you—remembering, of course, the cumulative sentence models you've learned—and then to compare your version of writeouts with the sentences as originally published. These "answers" are found in the Answer Key.

The point of such practice is not to "match" the original version. You'll profit simply by noting how your sentence decisions both parallel and differ from a modern writer's choices. If you're thoughtful in your combining, you may on occasion produce sentences that your professional competitor would envy. Obviously, you should resist the temptation to consult the original version *before* doing your combining work.

from "Death of a Pig" by E. B. White

It was a Saturday morning.

I found the gravediggers at work.
They worked in a thicket.
The thicket was dark and warm.
The sky was overcast.

Here Lennie had dug a beautiful hole.
The hole was among alders and young hackmatacks.
It was at the foot of the apple tree.
It was five feet long.
It was three feet wide.
It was three feet deep.

He was standing in it.
He was removing the last spadefuls of earth.
Fred patrolled the brink.
Fred made simple but impressive circles.
Fred disturbed the loose earth of the mound.
The earth trickled back in.

There had been no rain in weeks.
The soil was dry and powdery.
This was even three feet down.

from "So Much Depends on a Red Tent" by Grace Butcher

I built a fireplace of stones.
I cooked.
I ate.
I then sat with a cup of my special mix.
The mix was hot chocolate and coffee.
I watched the sun set.
I watched the tide come in.

I had been sitting in the dark.
I had been sitting on the red-brown sand.
My back was against the smoothness of the tree trunk.
The smoothness was water-washed.

But gradually I slumped farther and farther down.
Just my head was against the tree.
My body relaxed in the sand.

My fire was only embers.
An orange crescent of moon had brightened.
This was with the approach of darkness.
The tide had come to within a few yards of my feet.

I lay there for a long time.
I scarcely moved.

I could not have been more content.

from *Abbey's Road* by Edward Abbey

The chuckwalla is a lizard.
It is big.
It is fat.
It is ugly.
It is remarkably stupid.

It is a vegetarian.
It grazes on leaves.
The leaves are those of desert plants.
The plants include brittlebrush.
The plants include creosote.

We saw dozens of chuckwallas.
They scurried out from hiding places.
The hiding places were perfectly good.
They rushed across our path.
They tried to hide again.
Their hiding was between or under rocks.
They dug in frantically.

The animal's defense seems to be the tail.
This defense is its only one.
The tail is heavy.
The animal switches it back and forth.
The switching is like a whip.

It is wedged in a crevice.
It puffs itself up.
It hopes to become inextricable.

from *Ordinary People* by Judith Guest

He is in an entry.
The entry is empty of people.
It is longer than it is deep.
It has a chair in it.
It has a floor lamp.
It has a small table.
The table is strewn with magazines.
It has a green metal wastebasket.

The room is barely furnished.
The room still seems cluttered.

Opposite him is a doorway.
A chair blocks it.
The chair is overturned.

Sounds are issuing from inside the other room.
The sounds are mysterious.
The sounds are shuffling.

He moves toward the door.
A scene confronts him.
The scene is total disorder.

from *Cosmos* by Carl Sagan

The Sun will slowly pulsate.
It will be in its death throes.
It will expand once every few millennia.
It will contract once every few millennia.
It will eventually spew its atmosphere into space.
The spewing will be in concentric circles of gas.
The circles will be one or more.

The solar interior will flood the shell with light.
The solar interior will be hot.
The solar interior will be exposed.

The light will be ultraviolet.
This will induce fluorescence.
The fluorescence will be a lovely red and blue.
It will extend beyond the orbit of Pluto.

Perhaps half the mass of sun will be lost in this way.

The solar system will then be filled with a radiance.
The radiance will be eerie.
The radiance will be the ghost of the Sun.
The ghost will be outward bound.

from "The Jockey" by Carson McCullers

The jockey had left the wall.
He was approaching the table.
The table was in the corner.

He walked with a prim strut.
He swung out his legs with each step.
The swinging was in a half-circle.
His heels bit smartly into the carpet on the floor.
The carpet was red velvet.

On the way over he brushed against a fat woman.
He brushed her elbow.
She was in white satin.
She was at the banquet table.
He stepped back.
He bowed with dandified courtesy.
His eyes were quite closed.

He had crossed the room.
He drew up a chair.
He sat at a corner of the table.
He sat between Sylvester and the rich man.
There was no nod of greeting.
There was no change in his face.
His face was set.
His face was gray.

from "The Keel of Lake Dickey"
by John McPhee

A day comes in spring.
The river's surface breaks into giant floes.
The surface is frozen.
The surface has been solid four or five months.
The floes begin to move downstream.

They weigh many tons.
They grind and screech.
They jam up in bends of the river.
Backrising water explodes them free.

Downriver move hills of ice.
The ice is avalanchine.
The ice is pale green.
The ice crashes.
The ice tumbles.
The ice tears the banks.
The ice splits the sunshine into rainbows.

Great pieces skid off the edges.
They come to rest on the forest floor.

All the way down, we have seen trees.
The trees are high above the river.
The trees have sapwood glistening.
Big blazes of bark have been torn away.
The ice has done the tearing.

from "Canadian Spring"
by Sheila Burnford

The frog activity is dying down.
Muskrats are suddenly busy.
The V of their wake spreads in the still water.
The water is close to shore.

Their little faces forge through the reeds.
Their faces are preoccupied.
Their faces are bewhiskered.

More ducks fly in.
They settle on the larger ice floes.
They preen themselves.
Their cheerful garrulity is suddenly silenced.
An osprey appears overhead.
It hovers watchfully.

They rise in a body.
They circle.
They rise and fall uneasily.
The hawk drifts off down the shoreline.
Its drift is on an eddy of wind.
Its drift is effortless as a feather.

EIGHT
MODEST BEGINNINGS

Combining work in this final section is much different from either the cued or open exercises that you've already encountered. Your task is to read through an exercise, answer questions that are posed for each base sentence, and then do combining. (The details that you generate are the ones you use as part of your writeout.)

For example, suppose that you see the following exercise:

> **A sound breaks the silence.**
> What kind of sound? .
> What is the sound like?
> Where is the silence?

By picturing a situation, you can invent a list of details for each question. It is from these words and phrases that you will construct both cumulative and noncumulative sentences—as the spirit moves you. For the above exercise, your writeout might look like this:

> **Like fingernails scraped across a chalkboard, a screeching sound breaks the silence in the metal shop—a grim, grimey place.**

The base sentences in these exercises have been organized to form the skeletons of descriptive and narrative paragraphs. To ensure that your final writeouts will coherently fit together, you should read the entire exercise *before* generating details for each cluster.

Concentrate on constructing a *balance* of cumulative and noncumulative sentences. You will find it interesting to compare your versions of these exercises with those done by other students—and to use the writeouts as springboards for on-your-own writing. Great writing can result from modest beginnings.

Feeling Hungry

I'm feeling hungry?
> How hungry?
> Why hungry?

I decide to make a sandwich.
> What size of sandwich?
> What kind of sandwich?

The refrigerator door swings open.
>What happens to the light?
>What does the light illuminate?

I push aside milk cartons?
>How many?
>What size?
>Why pushed aside?

Finally I find what I'm looking for.
>List the items.

Followup: Describe step-by-step the sandwich that you make.

Mystery

It is nearly 3:00 A.M.
>Where?
>What is it like?

The house is still.
>What kind of house?
>Still except for what?
>Completely dark?

A door eases open.
>In what manner?
>Any noise?
>Any light?

The door closes.
>Any noise?
>What happens to the light?

A figure moves across the room.
>What sort of figure?
>What kind of movement?
>In what direction?

Followup: Narrate what happens next in this story.

Sitting at My Desk

I sit at my desk.
   List what you see.

My mind is filled with words.
   Why?

I can hear others around me.
   Name the others.
   What are they doing?

Writing sentences like this is easy.
   Why?

I am becoming my pen.
   What is your pen doing?

My voice trickles down my arm.
   Where does it go?
   What does it leave behind?

Followup: Describe what writing *feels* like as you do it.

Playoff Game

Jason shovels a pass to Willie.
   What kind of pass?
   What is Willie doing?

The seconds are ticking down.
   What is the crowd doing?
   Why?

Willie fakes toward the basket.
   How does he fake?
   What does he then do?

He goes up in a motion.
   What kind of motion?
   Where is the ball?

It flicks toward the basket.
What happens to it?

The crowd screams.
Why?

Followup: Narrate the action of this playoff game.

Saturday Night

It's Saturday night.
>Where?
>Describe the place you've named.

Young people are on the streets.
>What are they doing?
>Why?

Cars cruise by.
>What other vehicles cruise by?
>What's the purpose of cruising?

A patrol car is part of the scene.
>Marked or unmarked car?
>Why is the patrol car there?

The police are maintaining a profile.
>What kind of profile?
>How are they doing this?

And then the inevitable happens.
>Name what happens.

Followup: Describe the scene that follows.

Road Bike

My motorcycle stands waiting at the curb.
>Old or new motorcycle?
>What kind?
>How is it parked?

Light plays down its flanks.
>Describe the light.
>What color are its flanks?

Its engine is gleaming silver.
>What else is silver (or chrome)?

Its seat is deeply-padded vinyl.
> What color is the seat?
> How is it designed?

This is a classic road bike.
> It is built for what?
> How is it equipped?

It looks more like a sculpture than a machine.
> What does the sculpture suggest?

Followup: Describe mounting and starting your motorcycle as part of a cross-country trip.

Suburban Cowboy

Nick Notsoquick swaggered into the cafe.
> Who was Nick Notsoquick?
> Where was he from?
> What sort of cafe?

His manner was self-assured.
> Any other kind of manner?

He was dressed in a cowboy hat.
> List four other items of apparel.
> Describe two of the items.

All of this clothing had just been purchased.
> Handsome or silly clothing?
> Expensive or inexpensive clothing?
> Where was it purchased?

Nick was doing his best to look like a cowboy.
> How did he stand?
> Where did he put his hands?
> How did he wear his hat?

Followup: Explain what Nick is up to in the cafe.

In School

The teacher stood before the class.
Who was the teacher?
Which class?
What was he or she doing?

Tension filled the room.
What was the tension like?

The teacher's question was repeated.
What sort of question?

How was it repeated?
Why was it repeated?

Students sat hunched at their desks.
What were the students doing?
What were the students not doing?

Moments passed.
How many?
What were the moments like?
How did they pass?

Finally one student raised a hand.
Who was the student?
How did he or she do this?
What else did he or she do?

Followup: Create a dialogue between the student and teacher.

ANSWER KEY

Your answers for exercises in sections A to H should be similar to the ones shown here. Some minor differences in punctuation or style are possible for cued exercises—items 1 to 10 in each sequence.

Answers for open exercises—items 11 to 20 in each sequence—may vary considerably, but all should conform to the model pattern. The original versions of sentences from "Eight Modern Writers" follow the answers for sections A to H.

As you compare your sentences with ones in the Answer Key, pay close attention to details of structure and punctuation. Don't consult the answers until you've made writeouts in your own notebook.

MODEL A

A•1 Terry glanced desperately at Tonya, looking for help on a question.

A•2 The player took the handoff, turning sharply, faking to the outside, rolling against tacklers.

A•3 The slender dancer was at the rain-smeared window, watching the traffic, thinking about her boyfriend.

A•4 Shouts echoed through the courtyard—shrill and discordant, full of churning emotion.

A•5 Lennon's music was a political force, a sensitive voice that spoke for millions.

A•6 Two girls elbow into line—their legs long, their skirts short, their talk slangy and bright.

A•7 We sat quietly in the oppressive darkness, huddled together for warmth, troubled by noises from outside.

A•8 The inexperienced job seeker comes in, blinking with embarrassment, licking his lips nervously, fumbling with words.

A•9 The flag is a symbol—a focus for social ceremonies, a means of momentarily uniting people.

A•10 The skier came over a low, choppy crest—her body crouched, her weight forward, one ski slightly ahead of the other.

A•11 The instructor approached our group, smiling affably, trying to look sincere.

A•12 Writing well requires effort, a sustained mental concentration.

A•13 The sky was a cobalt blue—utterly clear, brutally cold.

A•14 She headed in his direction—her walk quick, her face angry.

A•15 Ours is a nation of hope, a land of opportunity for homeless immigrants.

A•16 The stranger moved into the brilliant sunshine—hands on his hips, a hat pulled low over his eyes.

A•17 And then shouts erupted—savage, bloodthirsty, full of hate.

A•18 Debbie inspects her mirror image, first puffing up her "beehive bouffant" hairdo, then replastering her ruby-red lipstick.

A•19 Intercontinental missiles nestle in their concrete silos both here and abroad—their systems programmed, their warheads armed.

A•20 Nurses have a highly demanding program of study, including course work, internships, and comprehensive examinations.

MODEL B

B•1 Closing his eyes, slumping at his desk, Mark hoped to catch a quick nap.

B•2 Rich with promise, abundant with opportunity, the future lies before us.

B•3 Suave, cunning, eager to make a buck, a salesman sidled near to his prey.

B•4 Her face angry, her mouth twitching in disgust, Molly defiantly stood her ground.

B•5 Careening out of the vacant lot, weaving from side to side, the car rumbled down the deserted alley.

B•6 Sparking with life, crackling with untried, untested possibilities, the present moment feels electric.

B•7 A defender of liberty, a spokesperson for minorities, a fiscal conservative, a friend of the environment, Senator Snort deserves your support.

B•8 Painted green and stuffed with scarred desks, the lecture hall was an institutional waiting room.

B•9 His body bent and frail, his walk shuffling and labored, the old man moved down the sidewalk.

B•10 Unaware of the danger that she would soon face, anxious to reach the summit, Jill climbed toward a rocky outcropping that was warmed by the sun.

B•11 Swaying dangerously, groaning in protest, the tree withstood high winds.

B•12 Quite elderly, unable to care for himself, Mr. Thomas finally moved to a retirement home.

B•13 An act of love, a gesture of kindness, the gift went unacknowledged.

B•14 One eye closed, the other squinting fiercely, Janice slowly squeezed the trigger.

B•15 Comfortable with sentence combining, eager to try my skills, I decided to make my own two-level sentence.

B•16 Working together, sticking to the business at hand, refusing to squabble, the committee soon finished its task.

B•17 Sincere in his efforts but misguided in his approach, the legislator campaigned on his remarkably ineffectual record and lost the election by a landslide.

B•18 A skilled craftsman, a fine athlete, and a terrific cook, George won a community award for being "well rounded."

B•19 Encouraged by gains during the civil-rights era, minorities have consolidated their clout and become a potent force in American politics.

B•20 Her voice lyrical and pure, her interpretation sensitive and compelling, the singer made her New York debut.

MODEL C

C•1 Jean—listening hard, hearing unusual noises—felt her pulse quicken.

C•2 Inflation—the devaluation of currency, the erosion of buying power—undermines the stability of government.

C•3 A study group—examining the problem, struggling with options—debates various possibilities.

C•4 Mud—warm and relaxing—oozed between her toes.

C•5 The quarterback—one arm cocked, the other extended for protection—drops back to pass.

C•6 Storm waves—exploding into foam, spewing white up the jagged cliffs—thundered against the rocks.

C•7 The cabin—damp, creaky, and badly in need of cleaning—now belonged to him.

C•8 The school's priorities—athletics, social events, a marching band—were clear to its staff.

C•9 Power lines—running parallel to the road, spanning gulches and rocky streambeds—stretch through the dessert.

C•10 The team captain—his neck reddened above his white collar, his muscular shoulders flexing for the girls—approached the podium.

C•11 The football, kicked end-over-end, took a great bounce in the wrong direction.

C•12 Our product—thoroughly tested, fully guaranteed—is ready to market.

C•13 The driver, glancing down carelessly and reaching for a cigarette, careened into the ditch.

C•14 A broken cup—its handle missing, its rim badly chipped—was all that remained.

C•15 Theresa, hearing about summer employment opportunities in national parks, headed for the campus job office.

C•16 The company's goals—reduced expenses, increased sales, and higher profits—have been achieved.

C•17 Many women, reluctant to give up careers and intellectual interests, share housework with their husbands.

C•18 American companies—responding to Japan's challenge and trying to re-gain leadership—are now producing cars that are highly fuel-efficient and much more reliable.

C•19 The hurricane—the second of the season, a storm with tremendous fury—gathered destructive force 500 miles offshore.

C•20 A group of coal miners—banners uplifted, arms locked together—marches in silent protest against safety conditions that demand attention.

MODEL D

D•1 Racing the engine, he slipped the machine into gear, backing carelessly across the sidewalk.

D•2 Wearing a school blazer, the coach stood before the crowd, grinning good naturedly.

D•3 Like flowers in a garden, fireworks blossomed briefly in space, the night sky above the river.

D•4 Down near the action, the reporter got out her notepad, ready to record the details.

D•5 Surprised by the turnout, they hesitated for a moment, hunched in the doorway.

D•6 The sky—an enormous blue hole—was edged by trees, a circle of green.

D•7 Hawkins—a lanky forward—angled toward the baseline, an unguarded area.

D•8 Golden and warm, the afternoon was like a dream, breathless with promise.

D•9 The room—a small vestibule—was decorated in yellows and earth tones, a happy mix of colors.

D•10 Clouds—gray and sullen on the horizon—had formed a storm front, ominous in its portent.

D•11 Listening to the cheers, Jeff stepped to the plate, eyeing the center-field bleachers.

D•12 Glad for the experience, I drove back home after the tournament, confident in my ability.

D•13 Flirting with disaster, the republic had overextended itself, borrowing at high interest rates.

D•14 With both arms extended, she vaulted across the balance beam, her timing perfect.

D•15 The bomb, a harmless-looking package, ticked away toward noon, the fateful hour that would wreak destruction.

D•16 The young woman—listless and distraught—appeared suicidal, unable to cope.

D•17 Nervous about their investment but reluctant to pull out their money, officials waited anxiously for news, hopeful for a major oil find.

D•18 The wrestler, a perfect villain, grinned at the crowd—a collection of farm hands who liked a good Saturday night show.

D•19 Her house—an old, brick Victorian that had begun to decay from neglect—was on the edge of town, a place where asphalt ended and crab grass took over.

D•20 Neither expecting nor wanting reprieve, the convict faced his death with dignity, trying to atone for his violent crimes that had caused much suffering.

MODEL E

E•1 The singer stepped into the footlights, grinning down at the girls, his mouth forming a kiss.

E•2 Election results come in slowly, the small precincts reporting first, providing data for predictions.

E•3 Dancers moved in syncopation, nodding and jerking, their faces transfixed.

E•4 The cat came with a leap, tan and tawny, springing on its prey.

E•5 She was tall and gaunt, shimmering in sequins—her face frozen in a waxy smile.

E•6 Mike lifted the copper-colored tone arm, its needle delicate, poised above the grooved record.

E•7 It was a sanctuary, a place of refuge—cool, quiet, away from telephones.

E•8 Most children begin school with enthusiasm—eager to learn, open to knowledge—literally hungering for intellectual stimulation.

E•9 Life is thin and tensile, a stream of consciousness sparking between Alpha and Omega, the positive and negative cosmic poles.

E•10 There was a single image—his father—heavy muscled, beaded with sweat, turning to smile and wave at him.

E•11 Our coach leaps from the bench, gesturing wildly at the referee, his face a portrait of anguish.

E•12 The moon hung in the night sky, a crescent of pale light, distant and sad.

E•13 Friends came in hordes, their voices full of cheer, singing ballads.

E•14 The commission was a public-relations effort, symbolic but meaningless, its recommendations a joke.

E•15 Sue stood in the lunch line, hungry for dessert, thinking about her commitment to lose weight.

E•16 Music is an escape—a magic journey that takes us into ourselves, providing a brief vacation.

E•17 Footsteps retreat slowly, scuffing across sandy, well-worn linoleum, their sound finally fading.

E•18 Then came an inane announcement, the fourth of the period, causing our instructor to groan and curse.

E•19 The carriage lumbers forward—its wheels glinting in the sun and its chassis straining under its load, a heap of badly rusted scrap metal.

E•20 The old barn shuddered, its walls buckling, collapsing with a roar as it sent up sparks in a shower—a flurry of fireflies, rising in the night.

MODEL F

F•1 Awake again, he squinted at the typewriter keys, knotted against the carriage roller.

F•2 Like wisps of cobweb, Rick's hair was combed straight back, giving him a severe appearance.

F•3 Dipping at the wind's bidding, the willows swayed dramatically, branches dancing in rhythm.

F•4 A rich mix of vegetables, the stew bubbled in the pot, attracting people by its smell.

F•5 Laughing wildly, two students waited at the bus stop—one swinging his arms in pantomime, the other making strange faces.

F•6 Making a neat trajectory, the paper ball bounced against overdue books, skittering into an open briefcase, a kind of wastebasket.

F•7 Grimy from hours on the road, the rig was parked near a café, its exhaust soot spreading in a black banner, feathering out near the rear door.

F•8 Alert and aggressive, Chris searches for answers, probing beneath the surface, seeking hidden truths.

F•9 Outdated by aircraft, expensive to operate, railroad passenger service must make changes, improving its coaches, serving good food, and treating its customers courteously.

F•10 Armed and ready, SAC is on twenty-four-hour alert, its planes lined up, its pilots directed toward targets, its backup systems in order.

F•11 Like money in the bank, a friendship is something you draw upon, helping you get through hard times.

F•12 Aging gracefully, the executive now seemed more relaxed, a little less defensive.

F•13 Easing light across the land, dawn came quietly in the east, its progress soft and inexorable.

F•14 Battered by recession, the economy finally began to regain strength, making investors feel more confident.

F•15 Eager to please his boss, the typist took evening classes, boosting his speed to 100 words per minute.

F•16 Hoping to get the contract, we presented our analysis, a projection of trends for consumer demand.

F•17 Devoid of ornament, the building was clean, angular, and contemporary—a stark glass box.

F•18 Out of breath and late again for class, I ran down the hallway that was now deserted, not knowing what to expect.

F•19 Leaning toward the camera, the thick-shouldered team captain stands at the sidelines—a roped-off area—looking shy and confused.

F•20 Huddled together, hands in their jackets, the women rocked with laughter, their voices loud and clear, sharing more than recipes.

MODEL G

G•1 The music was loud, glittering with guitars, and the dancers moved with the sound—their bodies jerking, their hips grinding and gyrating, their feet pawing the floor.

G•2 Docile and passive, some students refuse to take responsibility for learning, and the system finally "educates" them—helping them to "adjust," encouraging them to "fit in" and not ask questions.

G•3 Smog hung over the city, choking off light from the sun, and all the heat—mixed with dirt and industrial waste—seemed trapped, making the air unbearable.

G•4 A beard keeps one's face warm—protecting one's face from the cold, shielding one's face from the wind—but it also attracts attention, sometimes lending credence to one's arguments.

G•5 Many of Sutton's poems are dead—his lines buried in geography, his words muffled in cliché—but this poem is alive and engaging, forcing the reader to listen and demanding a response.

G•6 The optimist sees things as hopeful and exciting, rich with promise, whereas the pessimist sees things as dark and impossible, hopelessly absurd.

G•7 Lifting into the horizon, the jet—a Boeing 747—powered upward, and then it banked to the east, its silver skin glinting, its shape getting smaller, its roar fading.

G•8 Everyone worked together—pushing in unison, rocking the car—and then it slowly began to edge forward, wheels spinning and catching hold, engine revving in unmuffled protest.

G•9 Working at odd hours, the poet pores over notebooks and through papers—trying to get organized, hoping for an idea—and sometimes the perfect sentence happens, a window into another universe.

G•10 A misfit, an oddball, and a crackpot, Norton tried to promote legislation for a 6:00 P.M. curfew, but his efforts were unsuccessful, thanks to a citizens' group that rose up in protest.

G•11 A voice spoke to him—soft and forgiving—but he hung up the phone without reply.

G•12 The signal changes color, and cabbies race to the next intersection, gunning their engines unmercifully and honking their horns.

G•13 Wanting to beat the crowds, hoping to get a front-row seat, we took a shortcut to the stadium—but so did everyone else in town.

G•14 Brutalized by war, the peasants desperately wanted peace, but their leaders—insulated from suffering—had other ideas.

G•15 Girls were lying on the grass, eating sandwiches and sipping milkshakes, and boys were swaggering down the walk, trying to look *macho*.

G•16 The officer stared straight ahead, assessing the threat, and then she moved down the aisle, her heels clicking on the tile, her weapon drawn.

G•17 Christmas is a time for joy, a season for giving, but for many it brings depression, an inner ache called loneliness.

G•18 Listening to the sermon, he mulled over its guilt-laden message; but the words seemed suddenly hollow, empty of meaning.

G•19 Unrestrained and jubilant, a shout went up from the crowd, and the marathon winner stumbled toward the finish—arms lifted in victory, tears streaming down her face.

G•20 The earth revolves around the sun, completing a cycle every 365¼ days, but it also rotates on its axis every 24 hours, giving us day and night, which is a framework for our lives.

MODEL H

H•1 Tony put his razor on the sink, a bowl of porcelain, shallow and squarish, and then he closed his eyes, cupping his hands together, splashing water on his face.

H•2 Intrigued by the grasshopper, Jennifer eyed it carefully, watching its struggle for escape, but then her mother—the voice of authority—called her to lunch, breaking the spell.

H•3 Loud and abrasive, a buzzer echoed up the hall, a signal for school to begin, and students raced for their classes, their shirttails flying, books tucked under their arms.

H•4 Praying for a reprieve, the teenager switched to the evasive tactics—including giggles and disjointed small talk—but the parent leaned forward, her manner insistent, probing for straight answers.

H•5 Dragging their gunny sacks, the clam diggers were ghostly shapes—their movements slow and meditative, hunched in the wind and fog—but all of this would change by noon, a rendezvous time for surfers.

H•6 Taking his leap, the diver sprang high into the air—his arms outstretched, his silhouette like a bird's—and then he tucked in a slow roll, his body in perfect rhythm, knifing the water.

H•7 Afraid of doing without, the pusher works the streets, hustling drugs to support his habit, and thus the circle of addiction widens, engulfing the young and enticing the gullible.

H•8 Churning with energy, the clouds come rolling in, sullen and dark, their shapes like mushrooms, and the wind becomes ominous, bringing a turbulent sound, a memory of other storms.

H•9 Hovering over the stove, her hair in curlers, Aunt Grace sets out her cup, measuring out a teaspoonful of instant coffee, and then she pours the water, a sizzling stream that consumes the crystals.

H•10 Compassion is such a simple act—a matter of smiling and listening, showing concern for another person or offering a helping hand—yet we often have trouble conquering the fears that keep us apart.

H•11 The coffee was now cold, and he pushed it across the counter, staring at its bracken color—a disagreeable brown.

H•12 Traffic moved smoothly until dusk, and then the winter storm hit, making the streets treacherous and inhospitable, a bonanza for tow-truck operators.

H•13 A feminist, Monique often attends rallies, speaking about women's issues, but she maintains a low profile at work, refusing to be baited into argument.

H•14 Upbeat, funny, and irreverent, the play rivets one's attention, provoking thought through humor, but it also allows one to relax.

H•15 He pulled out on the highway, waiting for the traffic to clear, and then he pushed on the accelerator, leaving two "autographs"—a familiar signature.

H•16 Children race across the field—shrieking, whooping wildly, glad to be on vacation—and then they hit the water, pelting each other with mud.

H•17 The engine, fueled by gasoline, converts combustion into energy, and the crankshaft transfers this energy—called "torque"—to the axle, making the wheels turn, causing the car to move.

H•18 Anxious to record their writing instructor's ideas, the students wait—their notebooks open, pencils poised—but unfortunately a substitute arrives.

H•19 Her confidence up, the batter tensed with anticipation, toeing the dust, and then she connected with a fast ball, sending it into left field—a game-winning hit.

H•20 Flicked sideways, the Frisbee soars—spinning in an upward trajectory, slicing the horizon—and then it hovers, silent and graceful, riding a puddle of air.

from "Death of a Pig" by E. B. White

It was a Saturday morning. The thicket in which I found the gravediggers at work was dark and warm, the sky overcast. Here, among alders and hackmatacks, at the foot of the apple tree, Lennie had dug a beautiful hole, five feet long, three feet wide, three feet deep. He was standing in it, removing the last spadefuls of earth while Fred patrolled the brink in simple but impressive circles, disturbing the loose earth of the mound so that it trickled back in. There had been no rain in weeks and the soil, even three feet down, was dry and powdery.

E. B. White, "Death of a Pig" reprinted in Louise Desaulniers, ed., *Highlights from 125 Years of the Atlantic* (The Atlantic Monthly Company, 1977), pp. 432–33.

from "So Much Depends on Red Tent" by Grace Butcher

I built a fireplace of stones, cooked, ate, then sat with a cup of my special mix of hot chocolate and coffee, watching the sun set and the tide come in.

I had been sitting in the dark, on the red-brown sand, my back against the water-washed smoothness of the tree trunk. But gradually I slumped farther and farther down till just my head was against the tree and my body relaxed in the sand. My fire was only embers, an orange crescent of moon had brightened with the approach of darkness, the tide had come to within a few yards of my feet. I lay there for a long time, scarcely moving. I could not have been more content.

Grace Butcher, "So Much Depends on a Red Tent," *Sports Illustrated,* February 3, 1975.

from *Abbey's Road* by Edward Abbey

The chuckwalla is a big, fat, ugly, remarkably stupid lizard. A vegetarian, it grazes on the leaves of such desert plants as brittlebush and creosote. We saw dozens of chuckwallas scurrying from perfectly good hiding places, rushing across our path and trying to hide again between or under rocks, digging in frantically. The animal's only defense seems to be the heavy tail, which it switches back and forth like a whip. Wedged in a crevice, it puffs itself up, hoping to become inextricable.

Edward Abbey, *Abbey's Road* (New York: E. P. Dutton, 1979), p. 74.

from *Ordinary People* by Judith Guest

He is in an entry, empty of people, longer than it is deep, with a chair in it, a floor lamp, a small table strewn with magazines, a green metal wastebasket. Barely furnished, the room still seems cluttered. Opposite him is a doorway; an overturned chair blocks it. From inside the other room, mysterious, shuffling sounds are issuing. A scene of total disorder confronts him as he moves toward the door.

Judith Guest, *Ordinary People* (New York: Random House, 1976), pp. 35–36.

from *Cosmos* by Carl Sagan

In its death throes, the Sun will slowly pulsate, expanding and contracting once every few millennia, eventually spewing its atmosphere into space in one or more concentric shells of gas. The hot, exposed solar interior will flood the shell with ultraviolet light, inducing a lovely red and blue fluorescence extending beyond the orbit of Pluto. Perhaps half the mass of the Sun will be lost this way. The solar system will then be filled with an eerie radiance, the ghost of the Sun, outward bound.

Carl Sagan, *Cosmos* (New York: Random House, 1980), p. 232.

from "The Jockey" by Carson McCullers

The jockey had left the wall and was approaching the table in the corner. He walked with a prim strut, swinging out his legs in a half-circle with each step, his heels biting smartly into the red velvet carpet on the floor. On the way over he brushed the elbow of a fat woman in white satin at the banquet table; he stepped back and bowed with dandified courtesy, his eyes quite closed. When he had crossed the room he drew up a chair and sat at a corner of the table, between Sylvester and the rich man, without a nod of greeting or a change in his set, gray face.

Carson McCullers, "The Jockey" from *The Ballad of the Sad Café* (Boston: Houghton Mifflin, 1955); reprinted in *Sports and Literature,* ed. Henry B. Chapin (New York: David McKay Co., 1976), p. 207.

from "The Keel of Lake Dickey" by John McPhee

A day comes in spring when the river's frozen surface, which has been solid four or five months, breaks into giant floes, and they begin to move downstream. Weighing many tons, they grind and screech and, in bends of the river, jam up until backrising water explodes them free. Downriver move hills of avalanchine ice, pale green, crashing, tumbling, tearing the banks, splitting the sunshine into rainbows. Great pieces skid off the edges and come to rest on the forest floor. All the way down, we have seen trees, high above the river, with sapwood glistening, big blazes of bark having been torn away by the ice.

John McPhee, "The Keel of Lake Dickey" reprinted in *Giving Good Weight* (New York: Farrar, Straus, Giroux, 1979), pp. 145–46.

from "Canadian Spring" by Sheila Burnford

The frog activity is dying down, but the muskrats are suddenly busy, the V of their wake spreading in the still water close to the shore, preoccupied, bewhiskered little faces forging through the reeds. More ducks fly in and settle on the larger ice floes, preening themselves, their cheerful garrulity suddenly silenced when an osprey appears overhead and hovers watchfully. They rise in a body and circle, rising and falling uneasily, until the hawk drifts off down the shoreline on an eddy of wind, effortless as a feather.

Sheila Burnford, "Canadian Spring" reprinted in Louise Desaulniers ed., *Highlights from 125 Years of the Atlantic* (The Atlantic Monthly Company, 1977), pp. 499–500.

ABOUT THE AUTHOR

William Strong teaches courses in writing, English methods, and secondary reading at Utah State University in Logan. He has also taught high school English in Portland, Oregon, and worked as a language arts consultant in eastern Idaho. His educational background includes bachelor's and master's degrees from Portland State College and the University of Oregon respectively; he was a TTT fellow at the University of Illinois, where he received a Ph.D. in English. In addition to journal publications, he authored *Sentence Combining: A Composing Book* (Random House, 1973); *Sentence Combining and Paragraph Building* (Random House, 1981), and co-authored *Facing Value Decisions: Rationale-Building for Teachers* (Wadsworth, 1976; Teachers College Press, 1982). He has been a speaker and workshop leader at many state, regional, and national meetings and a consultant for several school districts. At present he directs the Utah Writing Project and edits the *Utah English Journal*.